ANSI C

PROGRAMMING CONCEPT

R. SIVARASAN M.Sc., M.Phil.,
LECTURER
GOVT. ARTS COLLEGE
KULITHALAI

First Edition: November 2016

© **Copy right reserved with Author & Publishers**

Designed and Printed By
Siva Offset & Screen Printers
Salem Main Road, Musiri,
Trihy – 621204
Cell – 9790484611

Price Rs   : 350 /-

ISBN-13: 978-1539725824

ISBN-10: 1539725820

Publishers:
Create Space
Amazon company , US

GOVT ARTS COLLEGE
KULITHALAI-639120

Prof. R.Govindaraj M.Sc.,MCA.,M.Phil.,PGDCA.,B.Ed.,Ph.D
E_mail: pr.govindaraj63@gmail.com
Phone: 9443581114

<u>FOREWORD</u>

I am very much pleased to note that Mr.R. SIVARASAN has brought out a book entitled "ANSI C PROGRAMMING CONCEPT".

C is one of the oldest languages. The language is basic foundation for all the languages, because the concept, structure and syntax are similar but the writing of code differs. Writing of code in other languages is based on the compiler of that language. Most of the students and teachers have to depend on books written by foreign authors. They may not be suitable to meet the needs of our students and teachers with respect to better understanding.

This book will strengthen the fundamentals of ANSI C language of both under graduate and post graduate students studying in professional computer science institution. The author himself actively involved in teaching C language and explained the various concepts in a simple way. It is a good effort that should be continued.

I wish that the author should bring out many literary contributions. I congratulate Mr.R. SIVARASAN for brought out such a useful book. I wish him all success in his future endeavors.

R. GOVINDARAJ

PREFACE

This text book is designed according to the new syllabus prescribed by the Bharathidasan University, Tiruchirappalli. While preparing this book, I have presented the subject matter in a very systematic and logical approach so as to make the content as simple as possible. This book is carefully written by getting feedback from the students. The author sincerely feels that the student community will be greatly benefited through this book.

The blessings and encouragements from the parents and friends are made to bring out this book successfully Above all, I thank God Almighty for giving inspiration and guidance in all stages of writing this book. Productive suggestions and constructive criticisms are most welcome.

October 2016

Mr. R. SIVARASAN

CONTENTS

1.1 INTRODUCTION TO C:

C is a popular general purpose, high-level programming language that was originally developed by Dennis M. Ritchie to develop the UNIX operating system at Bell Labs. C was orininally first implemented on the DEC PDP-11 computer in 1972.

The UNIX operating system and virtually all Unix applications are written in the C language. C has now become a widely used professional language for various reasons.

The history and development of C is illustrated.

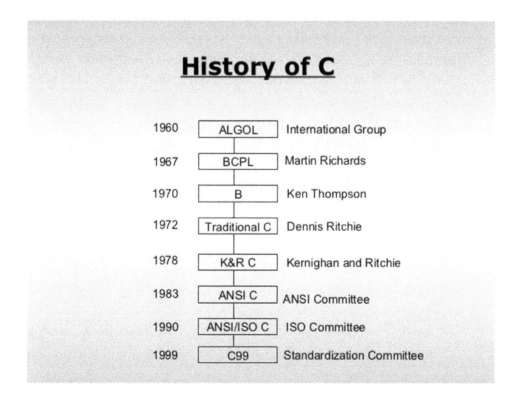

ANSI C STANDARD:

For many years there was no standard version of 'C' language. Due to this reason, portability feature of 'C' language was not provided from one computer to another computer. To overcome this discrepancy a committee was set up in the summer of 1983 to create a standard C version tha is popularly known a ANSI(American National standard Institute) STANDARD. The ANSI C standard was adopted in December of 1989 and the first copy of c language was introduced in the market in 1990. Today all compilers of C support to ANSI standard.

1.2 OVERVIEW OF COMPILERS AND INTERPRETERS

A program is a set of instructions for performing a particular task. These instructions are just like English words. The computer interprets the instructions as a 1's and 0's. A program can be written in assembly language as well as high level language. This written program is called as source program. The source program is to be converted to the machine language, which is called as object program. Either an interpreter or a compiler will do this activity.

a) *Interpreters*
   ✓ An Interpreter reads only one line of a source program at a time and converts it to object codes. In case of any errors, the same will be indicated instantly.
   ✓ The program written with an interpreter can easily be read and understood by the other users as well. So security is not provided. Anyone can modify the source code.
   ✓ Hence it is easier than compilers. But the disadvantage is that it consumes more time for converting a source program to an object program.

b) *Compilers*
   ✓ A compiler reads the entire program and converts it to the object code.
   ✓ It provides errors not of one line but errors of the entire program. Only error free programs are executed. It consumes little time for converting a source program to an object program.

✓ When the program length for any application is large, compilers are preferred.

1.3 BASIC STRUCTURE OF C PROGRAM,S.

Every C program contains a number of several building blocks known as functions. Each function of it performs task independently. A function is subroutine that may consist of one or more statements. A C program comprises of the following sections.

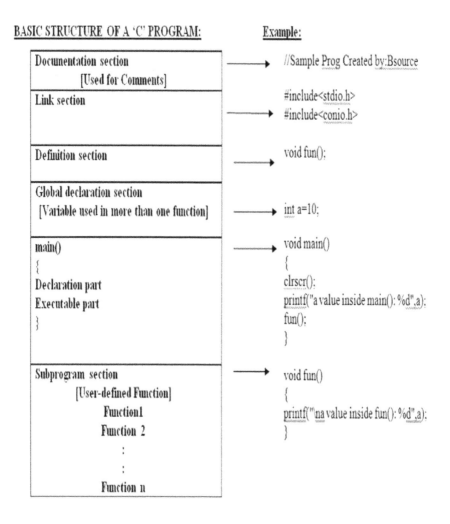

BASIC STRUCTURE OF A 'C' PROGRAM: Example:

| Documentation section [Used for Comments] | → | //Sample Prog Created by:Bsource |

Link section → #include<stdio.h>
#include<conio.h>

Definition section → void fun();

Global declaration section
[Variable used in more than one function] → int a=10;

main()
{
Declaration part
Executable part
}

→ void main()
{
clrscr();
printf("a value inside main(): %d",a);
fun();
}

Subprogram section
[User-defined Function]
Function1
Function 2
:
:
Function n

→ void fun()
{
printf("\na value inside fun(): %d",a);
}

Include Header File Section:

C program depends upon some header files for function definitionthat are used in program. Each header file by default is extended with . h. The file should be included I #include directive as given below.

Example:

 # include <stdio.h> or # include "stdio.h."

In this example <stdio.h> file is included i.e. all the definitions and prototypes of function defined £je are available in the current program. This file is also compiled with original program.

Global Declaration:

This section declares some variables that are used in more than one function. these variable are known as global variables. These variables must be declared outside of all the

Function Main:

Every program written in C language must contain main () function. Empty – parenthesis after main are necessary. The function main () is the starting point of every 'C' program. Mi: n of the program always begins with the function main (). Except the main () function, other sections may not be necessary. The program execution starts with the opening brace ({) K with the closing brace (}). Between these two braces the programmer should declare the and the executable part.

Declaration Part:

The declaration part declares the entire variables that are used in executable part. The initialization of variables is also done in this section. The initialization means providing to the variables.

Executable Part:

This part contains the statements following the declaration of the variables. This part contains **a** set of statements or a single statement. These statements are enclosed between

-

User-defined function:

The functions defined by the user are called user-defined functions. These functions are generally defined after the main () function. They can also be defined before main ( ) function. This portion is not compulsory.

Comments:

Comments are not necessary in the program. However, to understand the flow of programs the programmer can include comments in the program. Comments are to be inserted by the programmer. It is useful for documentation. The clarity of the program can be followed if it is documented.

Comment are nothing but some kind of statements which are placed between the delimiters /* & */. The Compiler does not execute comments. Thus, we can say that comments are not the part of executable program.

Basic Rule for writing C Programming:

1. In separate statement each instruction should be written. Therefore, complete C program consist of set of instructions.
2. The statements in program must be written in sequencial order to get desired output. Unless any logic problem can be arise.
3. All statement should written in small case letters.
4. C has no particular rules for position at which statement is to be typed.
5. In C program every statement must end with ; (semicolon).It act as a terminator.
6. Comment in the program should be enclosed within /* .. */ .Look example below the first line is comment.
      For ex. /*This my first program*

7. Main :
      main() is a collection of the set of statements. Statements are always enclosed belongs to main() within pairs of {} (opening and closing braces).For ex.
                  void main()
                  {
                    1st statement;
                    2nd statement;
                  }

8. Declaration:

    Any variable used in the program must be declared before using it. For ex,

    int a,b,c;   /*declaration*/

    a=a+b;   /*usage*/

9. For input use scanf("%d,%f",&a,&c); function i.e syntax is scanf("< string1>,< string2>,...",&variable1 ,&variable2..);

10. For output use printf("%d,%f",&a,&c); function i.e syntax is printf("<string1>,< string2>",variable1,variable2); , & is used in scanf function is must because it is "Address of operator". It gives the location number used by variable.

11. Linking:

    #include<stdio.h> stands for standard input output,

    #include<conio.h> stands for control input output. These are most commonly used for Linking.

1.4 EXECUTING THE PROGRAM:

The following steps are essential in executing a program in c.

1) Creation of Program

Programs should be written in C editor. The file name can be consist of letters, digits program include extension C.

Syntax: Hello_World . c

2) Compilation and Linking of a Program

The source program statements should be translated into object programs which is suitable for execution by the computer.

Linking

The translation id done after correcting each statement. If there is no error compilation proceeds and translated program is stored in another file with the same file name with extension ". obj".

Syntax: gcc Hello_World.c

3) Executing the Program

After the compilation the executable object code will be loaded in the computer's main memory and the program is executed.

Syntax: . / a . out

```
rajesh@Rajesh-Laptop:~$ gcc Hello_World.c
rajesh@Rajesh-Laptop:~$ ./a.out
Hello World
rajesh@Rajesh-Laptop:~$
```

Windows system

Step 1: Locate the TC.exe file and open it. You will find it at location **C:\TC\BIN\.**

Step 2: File > New (as shown in above picture) and then write your C program

```c
#include<stdio.h>
int main()
{
    printf("hello World!");
    return 0;
}
```

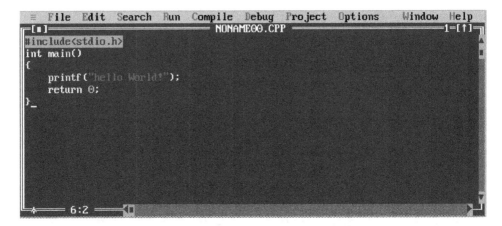

Step 3: Save the program using F2 (OR file > Save), remember the extension should be ".c". In the below screenshot I have given the name as helloworld.c.

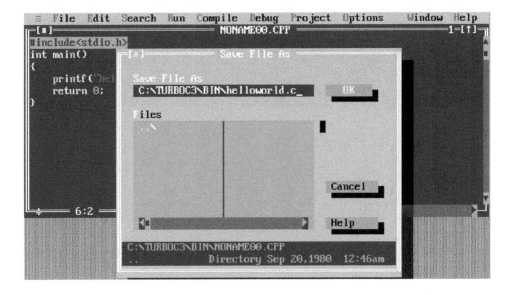

Step 4: Compile the program using Alt + F9 **OR** Compile > Compile (as shown in the below screenshot).

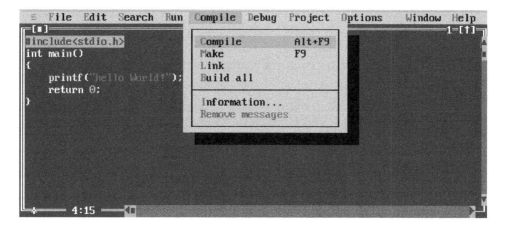

Step 5: Press Ctrl + F9 to Run (or select Run > Run in menu bar) the C program.

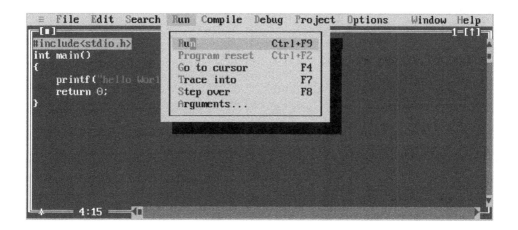

Step 6: Alt+F5 to view the output of the program at the output screen.

1.5 C TOKENS:

- ✓ A tokens is an individual words and punctuation marks are called token.
- ✓ More than on token can appear in a single line separated by white spaces.
- ✓ White space may be blank, carriage return or tab

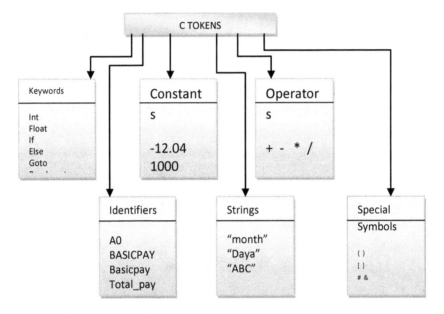

1.5.1 KEYWORDS:

- ✓ All keywords have fixed meanings and these meanings cannot be changed.
- ✓ Its serve as basic building blocks for program statements
- ✓ Keywords should be written in lowercase.

auto	float	signed	for	sizeof	break	friend
static	case	goto	switch	catch	if	template
char	inline	class	this	int	const	long
throw	continue	new	try	default	operator	typedef
void	if	else	short	double	public	virtual
enum	return	volatile	while	extem	register	union

1.5.2 IDENTIFIERS:

Identifiers are names given to variables, functions, arrays and other user defined objects. These are user defined names.

Rules:

1) Identifiers are formed with alphabets, digits and a special character underscore (_).
2) The first character must be an alphabet (or underscore).
3) Only first 31 characters are significant.
4) Cannot use a keyword.
5) Must not contain white space.

Example:

Valid identifiers: Basic, pay, CB02, TOTAL, B21, _TOTALPAY

Invalid identifiers:

Variable	Reason For Invalidity
AB.	Special character period (.) not allowed
9CB	The first character must be an alphabet
Auto	Reserve word

1.5.3 CONSTANTS:

✓ C Constants are also like normal variables. But, only difference is, their values can not be modified by the program once they are defined.
✓ Constants refer to fixed values. They are also called as literals
✓ Constants may be belonging to any of the data type.

✓

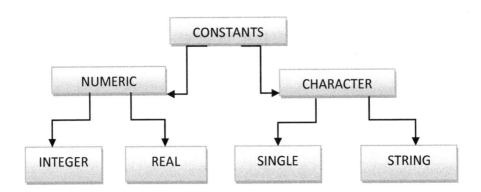

1.5.3..1 Integer Constants:

- ✓ An integer constant must have at least one digit.
- ✓ It must not have a decimal point.
- ✓ It can either be positive or negative.
- ✓ No commas or blanks are allowed within an integer constant.
- ✓ If no sign precedes an integer constant, it is assumed to be positive.
- ✓ The allowable range for integer constants is -32768 to 32767.

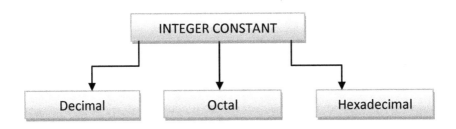

Type Of Integer Constants:

Decimal integers

Combination of Digits ⟹ 0 through 9, preceded by an optional - or + sign.

Total digits ⟹ decimal constant contain 10 digits only

Valid example ⟹ 142   -423   0   +432

Invalid example ⟹ 50,000 $300   2 500

Octal integers:

Combination of Digits ⟹ 0 Through 7

Total digits ⟹ octal constant contain 8 digits only

Valid example ⟹ 321   44   0   0543

Invalid example ⟹ 932   2198   8

Hexadecimal integers:

Combination of Digits ⟹ 0 Through 9, preceded by 0x (or) 0X

Combination of alphabet ⟹ A To F (A through F represent the no 10 through 15

Total digits ⟹ Hexadecimal constant contain 16 digits.

Valid example ⟹ 0X3F44 0x92 0xc12

1.5.3.2 Real constants:

The numbers containing fractional parts like 2.425. Such numbers are called Real or Floating point constants. A real number may also be expressed in exponential.

Valid example:

0.01342   +9.249   -0.0008 ⟹ Normal Type of real constants

0.24e3   5.91E+5   -3.16E-3 ⟹ Exponential Type of real Constants.

1.5.3.3 Single Character Constants:

A single character enclosed within a pair of single quote marks is called Single character constants. Character constants have integer values known as ASCII values.

Note: character constant '65' is not the same as the number 65

Printf("%d",'A'); ⟹ print the number 65 , the ASCII value of the letter A

Printf("%c", '65'); ⟹ print the alphabet character A

1.5.3.4 String Constants:

A sequence of characters enclosed in *double quotes* is called String Constants. The characters may be letters, numbers, special characters and blank space.

VALID EXAMPLE: ⟹ "WELCOME"   "A+B"   "326"
                        "A/B="   "A"

INVALID EXAMPLE ⟹ 'HELLO' 'A&B'   X

NOTE: character constant   [E.g. 'A'] is not equivalent to the single character string constant [E.g "A"].

Backslash Character Constants:

Backslash Character	Output functions
'\0'	Null
'\?'	Question mark
'\\'	Backslash
'\''	Single quote
'\a'	Audible alert
'\b'	Back space
'\n'	Ne line
'\t'	Horizontal tab

| '\r' | Carriage return |
| '\f' | Form feed |

1.6 Variables:

A variable is a data name that may be used to store a data value. Constant that remain unchanged during the execution of a program, a variable may take different value at different times during execution.

Variable name can be chosen by the programmer in a meaningful way so as to reflect its function or nature in the program.

Rules for naming C variable:
1. Variable name must begin with letter or underscore.
2. Variables are case sensitive
3. They can be constructed with digits, letters.
4. No special symbols are allowed other than underscore.
5. It should not be a keyword

Valid variable name: ⟹ E_name sum mark TOTAL Average john

Invalid variable name: ⟹ 123 (average) @name 1st

1.6.1 Declaring & Initializing Variable:

✓ Variables should be declared in the C program before to use.
✓ Memory space is not allocated for a variable while declaration. It happens only on variable definition.
✓ Variable initialization means assigning a value to the variable.

S.No	Type	Syntax	Example
1	Variable declaration	data_type variable_name;	int x, y, z; char flat, ch;
2	Variable initialization	data_type variable_name = value;	int x = 50, y = 30; char flag = 'x', ch='l';

1.6.2 Types of Variables
1. Local variable
2. Global variable
3. Environment variable

1. Local Variable:
- ✓ The scope of local variables will be within the function only.
- ✓ These variables are declared within the function and can't be accessed outside the function.
- ✓ In the below example, m and n variables are having scope within the main function only. These are not visible to test function.
- ✓ Like wise, a and b variables are having scope within the test function only. These are not visible to main function.

Example:
```
#include<stdio.h>
void test();
int main()
{
int m = 22, n = 44;        /* m, n are local variables of main function
                           m and n variables are having scope within
                           this main function only.These are not visible
                           to test funtion.
                           If you try to access a and b in this function,
                           you will get 'a' undeclared and 'b' undeclared
                           error */
printf("\n values : m = %d and n = %d", m, n);
test();
}
```

2. Global Variable:
- ✓ The scope of global variables will be throughout the program. These variables can be accessed from anywhere in the program.
- ✓ This variable is defined outside the main function. So that, this variable is visible to main function and all other sub functions.

Example

```
#include<stdio.h>
void test();
int m = 22, n = 44;
int a = 50, b = 80;
int main()
{
printf("All variables are accessed from main function");
printf("\nvalues: m=%d:n=%d:a=%d:b=%d", m,n,a,b);
test();
}
```

3. Environment Variables:

✓ Environment variable is a variable that will be available for all C applications and C programs.

✓ We can access these variables from anywhere in a C program without declaring and initializing in an application or C program.

✓ The inbuilt functions which are used to access modify and set these environment variables are called environment functions.

1.7 DATA TYPES:

C data type can be classified as

1. Basic data type
2. User defined data type
3. Derived data type

1.7.1 Basic Data Type

These data types are already defined in the language. They are

1. Char
2. Int
3. Float
4. Double

The following keywords are prefixed with the basic data types to produce new data types. These keywords are otherwise called as modifiers.

1. Signed
2. Unsigned
3. Long
4. Short

Note: These are used only with the basic data types int and char. Long can be used with double.

Type	Storage size	Value range
Char(or) signed	1 byte	-128 to 127 or 0 to 255
unsigned char	1 byte	0 to 255
int	2 or 4 bytes	-32,768 to 32,767 or -2,147,483,648 to 2,147,483,647
unsigned int	2 or 4 bytes	0 to 65,535 or 0 to 4,294,967,295
short	2 bytes	-32,768 to 32,767
unsigned short	2 bytes	0 to 65,535
long	4 bytes	-2,147,483,648 to 2,147,483,647
unsigned long	4 bytes	0 to 4,294,967,295
float	4 byte	1.2E-38 to 3.4E+38
double	8 byte	2.3E-308 to 1.7E+308
long double	10 byte	3.4E-4932 to 1.1E+4932

Special basic data type:

Void is a special basic data type. The compile will not allocate any memory special for this data type. This data type is used to

1) Define the functions.
2) Define the parameter passing
3) Define Pointers to void

1) Function returns as void

There are various functions in C which do not return any value or you can say they return void. A function with no return value has the return type as void.

For example, void exit (int status);

2) Function arguments as void

There are various functions in C which do not accept any parameter. A function with no parameter can accept a void.

For example, int rand(void);

3) Pointers to void

A pointer of type void * represents the address of an object, but not its type.

For example, a memory allocation function **void *malloc(size_t size);** returns a pointer to void which can be casted to any data type.

1.7.2 USER DEFINED DATA TYPES:

User defined data types are data types defined by the user. They are
1) Enumeration
2) Structure

1) Enumeration

This allows us to define our own data type with predefined values.

Syntax

> enum userdefined_name{ value1, value2, …….. value n };

Where

enum	⟹	keyword
userdefined_name	⟹	valid c name
value1 value2 value n	⟹	list of constants and are clled members internally these are treated as integers. That is value 1 = 0, value 2 = 1…… value n = n-1.

Example:

To define a variable which can take values as Jan, Feb, Mar,… Dec

Definition

enum month{ Jan,Feb,Mar,Apr,……..Dec};
internally Jan=0, Feb=1, Mar=2,……. Dec=11 will be stored.

2) Structure:

A structure is defined as data type to represent different type of data with a single name. The data items in a structure are called members of the structure

Defining a structure:

A structure definition contains a keyword struct and user defined tag-field followed by the members of the structure within braces.

Syntax:

```
struct tag-field
    {
        datatype member1;
        datatype member2;
        - - - - - - - - -
        ----------------
        datatype member n;
    }
```

Example:

Consider student information consisting of number, age, sex. The structure definition can be done as follows

```
struct student
    {
        int number;
        int age;
        char sex;
    };
```

Three members namely number, age and sex of different data types. The name of the structure is student.

1.7.3 Derived Data Types:

Derived data types are data type derived from existing data type such as basic data types or user defined data types. They are

1) Arrays
2) Pointer
3) Function

Array: An array is a fixed size sequenced collection of element of the same data type

Pointer: pointer is a memory variable that stores a memory address.

Function: a self-contained block or sub program of one or more statements that performs a special task when called.

1.8 symbolic constant :

✓ A *symbolic constant* is an "**variable**" whose value does not change during the entire lifetime of the program...
✓ Some constants in Mathematics:

Name of the constant	Value of the constant
Pi	3.1415926535...
e (Natural log)	2.718281828...

✓ Some constants in Phisics:

Name of the constant	Value of the constant
Gravitational Constant	6.67300×10^{-11} (m^3 kg^{-1} s^{-2})
c (speed of light)	299,792,458 (m/sec)

Why use symbolic constants ?

✓ It is generally a bad idea to write a constant out in a computer program each time that the constant is used:
  ○ It is prone to error
  ○ It is not convenient
✓ Consider the following program that computes the area of 2 circles:

```
public class Circle1
{
```

```
public static void main(String[] args)
{
    double r1 = 3.4;   // Radious of first cicle
    double r2 = 5.4;   // Radious of second cicle

    double area1;      // Area of circle 1
    double area2;      // Area of circle 1

    area1 = 3.1415926535 * r1 * r1;
    area2 = 3.1415926535 * r2 * r2;
} }
```

- ○ You can easily mistype a digit of Pi...
- ○ You have to remember the digits of Pi...
- ✓ So it is more convenient to give a name to a constant.
  This name assigned to a constant is then called a symbolic constant

1.9 OPERATORS:

An operator is a symbol that tells the computer to perform certain mathematical or logical manipulations.

TYPE OF OPERATORS:

S.NO	OPERATORS NAME	OPERATORS SYMBOL
1	Arithmetic Operators	+ - * / %
2	Relational Operators	< <= > >= == !=
3	Logical Operators	&& || !
4	Assignment Operators	+= -= *= /= %=
5	Increment and Decrement Operators	++ --
6	Conditional Operators	? :
7	Bitwise Operators	& | ^ << >>
8	Special Operators	sizeof() & * ,

1.9.1ARITHMETIC OPERATORS:

Symbol	Meaning
+	Addition or Unary plus
-	Subtraction or Unary minus
*	Multiplication
/	Division
%	Modulo Division

Syntax:

Operand   symbol   Operand

Where: Operand ⇒ A to Z (English alphabet character OR numbers)

Example: A + B   C – D   A / C   5 * 5

Types of arithmetic operators:

1) **Integer Arithmetic** ⟹ always yields an Integer value.
   [Ex: c=4 d=6   result of expression   a* b = 24]

2) **Real Arithmetic** ⟹ Use only real operands is called real arithmetic. Values either in decimal or exponential notation.
   [Ex: z = 20.5 / 4.5   = 4.555556]

3) **Mixed – Mode** one operands is integer and other is real, the expression is called a mixed mode arithmetic expression
   [Ex: 22 / 6.4 = 3.43] [15 / 10.0 = 1.5]

1.9.2 RELATIONAL OPERATORS:

Two quantities and depending on their relation, take certain decisions. These comparisons can be done with the help of Relational operators.

Symbol	Meaning
<	Less than
>	Greater than
<=	Less than or equal to
>=	Greater than
= =	Equal to
!=	Not equal to

Syntax:

Operand symbol Operand

Example: Relational expression
        C > D   OR   15 > 5

Result: The value of a relational expression is either One [or] Zero.

One ⟹ It is one if the specified relation is True

Zero ⟹ It is Zero if the specified relation is False.

1.9.3 LOGICAL OPERATORS:

We want to test more than on condition and make decisions use logical operators.

Symbol	Meaning
&&	Logical AND
||	Logical OR
!	Logical NOT

Syntax

| Expression 1 | Logical operators | Expression 2 |

Operator	Description	Example
&&	Called Logical AND operator. If both the operands are non-zero, then the condition becomes true.	(A && B) is false.
||	Called Logical OR Operator. If any of the two operands is non-zero, then the condition becomes true.	(A || B) is true.
!	Called Logical NOT Operator. It is used to reverse the logical state of its operand. If a condition is true, then Logical NOT operator will make it false.	!(A && B) is true.

1.9.4 ASSIGNMENT OPERATORS:

Assignment operators are used to assign the result of an expression to variable.

Syntax :

| v op = exp;   [or]   v = v op (exp); |

Operator	Description	Example
=	Simple assignment operator. Assigns values from right side operands to left side operand	C = A + B will assign the value of A + B to C
+=	Add AND assignment operator. It adds the right operand to the left operand and assign the result to the left operand.	C += A is equivalent to C = C + A
-=	Subtract AND assignment operator. It subtracts the right operand from the left operand and assigns the result to the left operand.	C -= A is equivalent to C = C - A
*=	Multiply AND assignment operator. It multiplies the right operand with the left operand and assigns the result to the left operand.	C *= A is equivalent to C = C * A
/=	Divide AND assignment operator. It divides the left operand with the right operand and assigns the result to the left operand.	C /= A is equivalent to C = C / A
%=	Modulus AND assignment operator. It takes modulus using two operands and assigns the result to the left operand.	C %= A is equivalent to C = C % A

1.9.5 INCREMENT AND DECREMENT OPERATORS:

The increment operator is written as ++ and the decrement operator is written as --.The increment operator increases the value of its operand by 1. The operand must have an arithmetic or pointer data type, and must refer to a modifiable data object. Similarly, the decrement operator decreases the value of its modifiable arithmetic operand by 1.

Syntax:

OP V ;   [OR]   V OP;

Example:

```
int  x;
int  y;
// Increment operators
x = 1;
y = ++x;    // x is now 2, y is also 2
y = x++;    // x is now 3, y is 2
// Decrement operators
x = 3;
y = x--;    // x is now 2, y is 3
y = --x;    // x is now 1, y is also 1
```

1.9.6 CONDITIONAL OPERATOR:

A ternary operator pair " ? : " is available in c to construct conditional expressions.

Syntax:

```
Exp1 ?   Exp2 :  Exp3 ;
```

Where Exp1, Exp2 , and Exp3 are Expressions.

The operator ? : works as follows: Exp1 is evaluated first. If is is nonzero(True), then the Exp2 is evaluated and becomes the value of the expression. If Exp2 is false, Exp3 is evaluated and its value becomes the value of the expression.

Operator	Description	Example
? :	Conditional Expression.	If Condition is true ? then value X : otherwise value Y

Example:

```
a=4  b=7;
X=(a>b) ? a : b ;
```

1.9.7 BITWISE OPERATORS

Bitwise operator works on bits and performs bit-by-bit operation. The truth tables for &, |, and ^ is as follows –

p	q	p & q	p | q	p ^ q
0	0	0	0	0
0	1	0	1	1
1	1	1	1	0
1	0	0	1	1

Assume A = 60 and B = 13 in binary format, they will be as follows –

$$A = 0011\ 1100$$
$$B = 0000\ 1101$$
$$\text{-----------------}$$
$$A\&B = 0000\ 1100$$
$$A|B = 0011\ 1101$$
$$A\char94 B = 0011\ 0001$$
$$\sim A = 1100\ 0011$$

The following table lists the bitwise operators supported by C. Assume variable 'A' holds 60 and variable 'B' holds 13, then –

1.9.8 SPECIAL OPERATORS:

Operator	Description	Example
sizeof()	Returns the size of a variable.	sizeof(a), where a is integer, will return 4.

&	Returns the address of a variable.	&a; returns the actual address of the variable.
*	Pointer to a variable.	*a;
,	Comma (link the related expression together	V=(a=2,b=7,a/b);

1.10 EVALUATION OF EXPRESSION:

Expressions are evaluated using an assignment statement of the form:

Syntax:

> Variable = expression ;

The statement is encountered, the expression is evaluated first and the result the replaces the previous value of the variable on the left hand side.

Priority

This represents the evaluation of expression starts from "what" operator.

Associativity

It represents which operator should be evaluated first if an expression is containing more than one operator with same priority.

Operator	Priority	Associativity
{}, (), []	1	Left to right
++, --, !	2	Right to left
*, /, %	3	Left to right
+, -	4	Left to right
<, <=, >, >=, ==, !=	5	Left to right
&&	6	Left to right
||	7	Left to right

| ?: | 8 | Right to left |
| =, +=, -=, *=, /=, %= | 9 | Right to left |

Example 1:

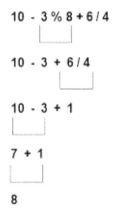

Rules

1) First, parenthesized sub expression from left to right are evaluated.
2) If parentheses are nested, the evaluation begins with the innermost sub-expression.
3) Arithmetic expressions are evaluated from left to right using the rules of precedence.
4) the expressions within parentheses assume highest priority

1.11 TYPE CONVERSIONS:

Type casting is a way to convert a variable from one data type to another data type. For example, if you want to store a 'long' value into a simple integer then you can type cast 'long' to 'int'. You can convert the values from one type to another explicitly using the **cast operator** as follows

There are two types of type casting

1.11.1. Implicit Conversion

✓ Implicit conversions do not required any operator for converted .
✓ They are automatically performed when a value is copied to a compatible type in program.

✓ Here, the value of a has been promoted from int to double and we have not had to specify any type-casting operator.This is known as a standard conversion.

✓ The **usual arithmetic conversions** are implicitly performed to cast their values to a common type. The compiler first performs *integer promotion*; if the operands still have different types, then they are converted to the type that appears highest in the following hierarchy –

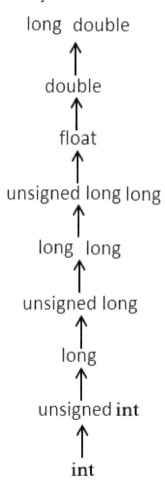

long double

↑

double

↑

float

↑

unsigned long long

↑

long long

↑

unsigned long

↑

long

↑

unsigned int

↑

int

Example :-

#include<stdio.h>

#include<conio.h>

void main()

```
{
    int i=20;
    double p;
    clrscr();
    p=i; // implicit conversion
    printf("implicit value is %d", p);
    getch();
}
```

Output:-

implicit value is 20.

1.11.2 Explicit Conversion:

✓ In c language , Many conversions, specially those that imply a different interpretation of the value, require an explicit conversion. We have already seen two notations for explicit type conversion.

✓ They are not automatically performed when a value is copied to a compatible type in program.

Example :-

```
#include<stdio.h>
#include<conio.h>
void main()
{
    int i=20;
    short p;
    clrscr();

    p = (short) i; // Explicit conversion
```

```
        printf("Explicit value is %d", p);

        getch();
    }
```

Output :-

Explicit value is 20.

2 DECISION MAKING STATEMENTS:

Decision making statements are used to skip or to execute a group of statements based on the result of some condition. The decision making statements are,

1) simple if statement
2) if.......else statement
3) nested if statement
4) switch statement

Rules

1) The brackets around the test condition are must
2) The test condition must be relational or logical expression
3) Statement block is called body of the if statement and it contains one or more statements.
5) The opening and closing brackets { } are must if the statement block contains more than one statement. Else optional.

2.1 SIMPLE IF STATEMENT:

Simple if statement is used to execute or skip one statement or group of statements for a particular condition. The general form is

Syntax:

> if(test condition)
> {
> statement block;
> }
> next statement;

When this statement is executed, the computer first evaluates the value of the test condition. If the value is true, statement block and next statement are executed sequentially. If the value is false, statement block is skipped and execution starts from next statement

Flow Diagram:

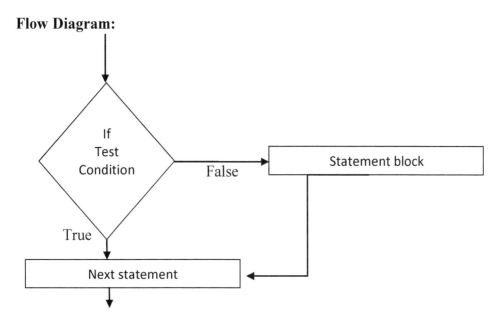

EXAMPLE

```
int main()
{
  int m=40,n=40;
  if (m == n)
  {
  printf("m and n are equal");
  }
}
```

OUTPUT:

m and n are equal

2.2 IF ELSE STATEMENT:

if........ else statement is used to execute one group of statements if the test condition is true or other group if the test condition is false. The general form is

Syntax:

```
if(test condition)
    {
        statement block-1;
    }
else
    {
        statement block-2;
    }
next statement;
```

When this statement is executed, the computer first evaluates the value of the test condition. If the value is true, statement block-1 is executed and the control is transferred to next statements' the value is false, statement block-2 is executed and the control is transferred to next statement.

Flow Diagram:

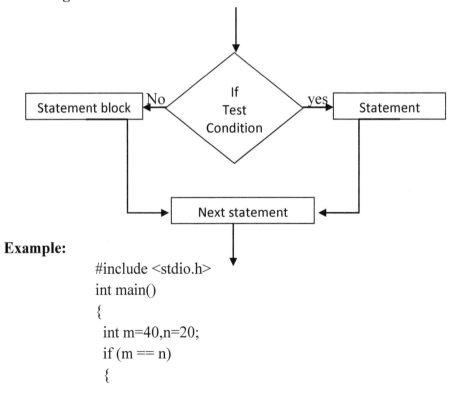

Example:

```
#include <stdio.h>
int main()
{
  int m=40,n=20;
  if (m == n)
    {
```

```
printf("m and n are equal");
}
else
{
printf("m and n are not equal");
}
}
```

OUTPUT:

```
m and n are not equal
```

2.3 NESTED IF STATEMENT

✓ In "nested if" control statement, if condition 1 is false, then condition 2 is checked and statements are executed if it is true.
✓ If condition 2 also gets failure, then else part is executed.

Syntax:

```
if(condition 1)
{
// statement(s);
}
else if(condition 2)
{
//statement(s);
}
.
.
.
.
else if (condition N)
{
//statement(s);
}
else
{
//statement(s);
}
```

The execution of a nested if-else statement, as soon as a condition is encountered which evaluates to true, the statements associated with that particular if-block will be executed and the remainder of the nested if-else statements will be bypassed. If neither of the conditions are true, either the last else-block is executed or if the else-block is absent, the control gets transferred to the next instruction present immediately after the else-if ladder.

Example

```
#include <stdio.h>
int main()
{
  int m=40,n=20;
  if (m>n) {
  printf("m is greater than n");
  }
  else if(m<n) {
  printf("m is less than n");
  }
  else {
  printf("m is equal to n");
  }
}
```

OUTPUT:

```
m is greater than n
```

2.4 SWITCH STATEMENT:

Switch statement is an extension of if else statement. This permits any number of branches. The general form is

Syntax:

switch(expression)

    {

case label-1:

        statement block-1;

        break;

case label-2:

        statement block-2;

        break;

case label-n:

        statement block-n;

        break;

default

        default statement;

        break;

    }

next statement

When this statement is executed the computer first evaluates the value of the expression in the keyword switch. This value is successively compared with the case label-1,label-2 label-n. If a case label matches with the value, the statement block associated with the case label is executed. Then the control is transferred to the next statement.

If none of the case matches with the value, the default statement block is executed.

Flow Diagram:

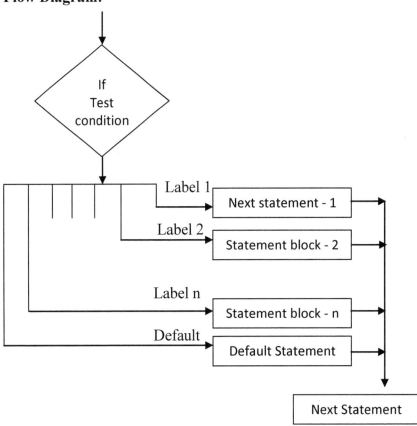

EXAMPLE:

```
#include<stdio.h>

int main( )
  {
  int day;
  printf("\n Enter the number of the day:");
  scanf("%d", &day);
  switch(day)
        {
        case 1:
                printf("Sunday");
                break;
        case 2:
                printf("Monday");
```

```
                        break;
            case 3:
                        printf("Tuesday");
                        break;
            case 4:
                        printf("Wednesday");
                        break;
            case 5:
                        printf("Thursday");
                        break;
            case 6:
                        printf("Friday");
                        break;
            case 7:
                        printf("Saturday");
                        break;
            default:
                        printf("Invalid choice");
                }
        return 0;

        }
```

Output:

Enter the number of the day   5

Thursday

2.5 LOOPING STATEMENTS:

Looping statements are used to execute a group of statements repeatedly until some condition is satisfied. The looping statements are

1) While statement
2) Do . . . . while statement
3) For statement

Rules:
1. The test condition should be any relational or logical expression enclosed within brackets.
2. If the body of the loop contains more than one statement, the { } brackets are must.

S.no	Loop Name	Syntax	Description
1	for	for (exp1; exp2; expr3) { statements; }	Where, exp1 – variable initialization (Example: i=0, j=2, k=3) exp2 – condition checking (Example: i>5, j<3, k=3) exp3 – increment/decrement (Example: ++i, j–, ++k)
2	while	while (condition) { statements; }	where, condition might be a>5, i<10
3	do while	do { statements; } while (condition);	where, condition might be a>5, i<10

2.6 WHILE STATEMENT:

- ✓ The while is an entry- controlled loop statement.
- ✓ The test condition is evaluated and if the condition is true, then the body of the loop is executed.
- ✓ if the condition is false, then the body of the loop will be skip.

The is a simple looping statement. The general form is.

Syntax:

```
while ( test condition )
{
body of the loop ;
}
next statement ;
```

The computer first evaluates the test condition. If the vale is false, the control is transferred to next statement. If the value is true, then the body of the loop is executed reputedly until the test condition becomes false. When the test condition becomes false the control is transferred to next statement.

Flow Diagram

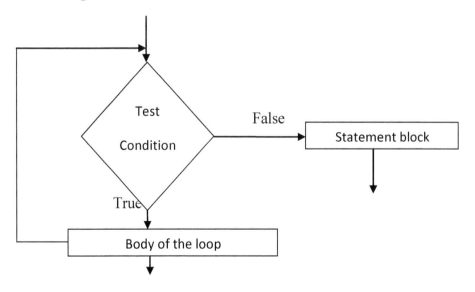

Example:

```
#include <stdio.h>
int main()
{
  int i=3;

  while(i<10)
  {
  printf("%d\n",i);
  i++;
  }
}
```

OUTPUT:

```
3 4 5 6 7 8 9
```

2.7 DO . . . . . . WHILE STATEMENT:

In do..while loop control statement, while loop is executed irrespective of the condition for first time. Then 2nd time onwards, loop is executed until condition becomes false.

Syntax:

```
do
{
body of the loop;
}
while ( test condition ) ;
next statement ;
```

When this statement is executed the body of the loop is executed first. Then the test condition is evaluated. If the value is false the control is transferred to the next statement. If the value is true the body of the loop is executed repeatedly until the test condition becomes false. When the test condition becomes false the control is transferred to the next statement.

Flow Diagram:

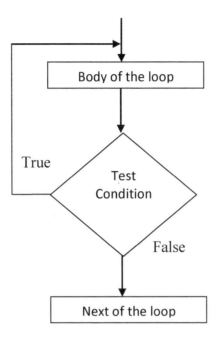

Example:

```
#include <stdio.h>
int main()
{
 int i=1;
  do
  {
  Printf("Display the values ");
   printf("Value of i is %d\n", i);
  i++;
  }while(i<=4 && i >=2);


}
```

OUTPUT:

> Display the values
> Value of i is 1
> Value of i is 2
> Value of i is 3
> Value of i is 4

2.8 FOR STATEMENT:

For statement is used to execute a statement or a group of statements repeatedly for a know number of times. The general form is

Syntax:

> For (initial condition ; test condition ; increment or decrement)
> {
> Body of the loop ;
> }
> Next statement ;

Where
1) Initial condition is used to set initial values to control variables.
2) Test condition is used to check the control variable. According to this the loop is executed or not
3) Increment or decrement is used to change the value of the control variable.

When the for statement is executed the value of the control variable is initialized and tested with the test condition. If the value of the test condition is true. The body of the loop will be executed and the control is transferred to the for statement. Then the value of the control variable is incremented or decremented. When the test condition becomes false the control is transferred to the next statement. The body of the loop is executed repeatedly as long as the test value is true.

FLOW DIAGRAM:

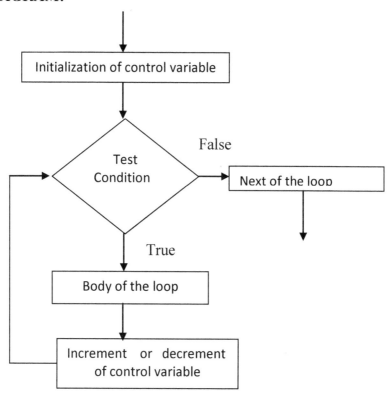

Example:

```
#include <stdio.h>

int main()
{
  int i;

  for(i=0;i<10;i++)
  {
     printf("%d ",i);
  }

}
```

OUTPUT:

```
0 1 2 3 4 5 6 7 8 9
```

ARRAY:

array is defined as a group of related data items that share a common name with different index values. The index value starts from 0 to n-1.

array_name[subscript];

where subscript - an integer from 0 to n.

Rules:
1) array_name must be valid C-variable name.
2) name of the array should be unique.
3) the elements in the array should be of same type
4) the subscript is always an integer
5) the subscript value cannot be negative.
6) The subscript must be given within square brackets after the array name.
7) if there are more than one subscript each should be given in separate square brackets.

3.1 SUBSCRIPT VARIABLES.

The variables which are used too represent the individual data in the memory are called subscripted variables.

Syntax:

array_name[subscript];

Example: a[7];

3.2 TYPE OF ARRAY:

The array can be classified as,
1. one dimensional array
2. two dimensional array
3. multi dimensional array

3.3 ONE DIMENSIONAL ARRAY:

An array name with only one subscript is known as on dimensional array.

Syntax: array_name[subscript]

Example:

1) a[3]

where:

a and ⟹ name of the arrays.

3 ⟹ is subscript data element or size of the array

2) grade[20]

grade ⟹ name of the arrays.

20 ⟹ is subscript data element
or size of the array

3.3.1 DECLARATION OF ONE DIMENSIONAL ARRAY:

array must be declared before it is used like other variables.

Syntax:

> **datatype array_name[size];**

Where

datatype ⟹ int float char etc.

array_name ⟹ variable name.

Size ⟹ number of contiguous location in the
memory to be reserved.

Example:

1) int mark[50];

This declares an integer type array named as **mark** having 50 memory location to store 50 integer data

2) char name[8]

This declares the name as a character array (string) variable that can hold a maximum of 8 characters. Suppose we read the following string constant into the string variable name.

"WELCOME"

each character of the string is treated as an element of the array **name** and is stored in the memory

'W'
'E'
'L'
'C'
'O'
'M'
'E'
'\0'

3.3.2 INITIALIZATION OF ONE DIMENSIONAL ARRAYS:

after an array is declared, its elements must be initialized. Otherwise, the will contain "garbage".

Syntax:

> **static datatype array_name[size]={ list of values};**

Where

static	$\Longrightarrow$	key word
datatype	$\Longrightarrow$	type of data found in the array such as int, float, char etc.
array_name	$\Longrightarrow$	variable name.
Size	$\Longrightarrow$	number of contiguous locations in the memory to be reserved.
List of values	$\Longrightarrow$	initial values to be given to the array. This should be separated by commas.

Example:

1) static float salary [ ] = {4.50,10.25,27.47,7.58};

      this declares salary as a real array and the size of the array is automatically allocated by counting the number of values. Here computer counts the value as four and assigns the size as 4.

salary[0]	salary[1]	salary[2]	salary[3]
4.50	10.25	27.47	7.58

2) static int age [6]={25,15,18,35};

      if the size of the array is grater than the number of values in the list, then the unused locations are filled with zeros as given below,

age[0]	Age[1]	Age[2]	Age[3]	Age[4]	age[5]
25	15	18	35	0	0

Example:

      write a program to find the smallest number and its position in a given one dimensional array.

```
#include<stdio.h>
void main()
{
    int I, j, n, small, pos;
    int a[50];
    printf("Give the vlaue of n");
    scanf("%d",&n);
    for(i=0; i<n; i++)
    sccanf("%d",a[i]);
    small=a[0];
    pos=0;
```

```
for (i=1; i<n; i++)

{

if (a[i] <= small)

    {

            small = a[i];

            pos= I;

    }

}

printf("The smallest element is :%d /n", small);

printf("The position is :%d /n", pos);

}
```

3.4 TWO DIMENSIONAL ARRAY:

an array with two subscripts is know as two dimensional array,

Syntax:

array_name[subscript 1][subscript 2]

where

subscript 1 $\Longrightarrow$ row number
subscript 2 $\Longrightarrow$ column number

Example:

A[2][2]

3.4.1 DECLARATION OF 2-D ARRAY:

Like one dimensional arrays two dimensional arrays must be declared before it is used like other variables.

Syntax:

datatype array_name[row size][column size];

Where

datatype	⟹	int, char, float etc.
array_name	⟹	variable name.
Row size	⟹	maximum number of rows in the table.
Column size	⟹	maximum number of column in the table.

Rules:

1) array_name must be valid C-variable name.

2) name of the array should be unique.

3) the elements in the array should be of same type

4) the subscript is always an integer

5) the size of the array is got by multiplying the row size and column size.

5) the subscript value cannot be negative.

6) The subscript must be given within square brackets after the array name.

Example

int mark [3][2];

	Column 0	Column 1
Row 0	Mark[0][0]	Mark [0][1]
Row 1	Mark [1][0]	Mark [1][1]
Row 2	Mark [2][0]	Mark [2][1]

The row number and column number mark[0][0] ...... mark[2][1] are called address of the locations.

3.4.2 ARRAY INITIALIZATION:

Like one dimensional arrays we can assign initialization values to 2-D arrays when they are declared.

Syntax:

static datatype array_name [row size][column size]={list of values};

where

static	⟹	key word
datatype	⟹	type of data found in the array such as int, float, char etc.
array_name	⟹	variable name.
Size	⟹	number of contiguous locations in the memory to be reserved.
List of values	⟹	initial values to be given to the array. This should be separated by commas.

Example:

static int mark[3][3]={8,2,9,28,34,43,15,20,5};

Mark[0][0]	Mark[0][1]	mark[0][2]
8	2	9
mark[1][0]	Mark[1][1]	mark[1][2]
28	34	43
mark[2][0]	mark[2][1]	mark[2][2]
15	20	5

This declares mark as an integer array having 3 row and 3 column. The total number of locations are 9 and these locations the values in the right hand side are stored as given below.

static int mark[2][2]={ {8,2},{7,10} };

This declares mark as an integer array having 4 location and assigns value

Mark[0][0]	Mark[0][1]
8	2
mark[1][0]	Mark[1][1]
7	10

Example:

write a program to read a n x m matrix.

```
#include<stdio.h>
void main()
{
int a[20][20] , I , j , m , n;
scanf("%d %d", &n,&m);
for ( i=0; i<n; i++ )
        for(j=0 ; j< m; j++)
                scanf(" %d", &a[i][j] );
}
```

3.5 MULTI-DIMENSIONAL ARRAYS:

an array with three or more subscripts is know as multi - dimensional array,

Syntax:

array_name[subscript 1][subscript 2]............. [subscript m];

where:

subscript 1 $\implies$ row number
subscript 2 $\implies$ column number

3.6 STRING HANDLING

a sequence of characters enclosed within double quotes are called string.

When a string is stored in the computer memory computer automatically places a null character '\0' as the last character or terminator.

The size of the string should be maximum number of characters in the string plus one.

3.6.1 DECLARING STRINGG VARIABLE:

a string variable should be declared as a character type array and is used to store string.

Syntax:

char variable_name[size];

where

char $\Longrightarrow$ datatype

variable_name $\Longrightarrow$ variable name.

Size $\Longrightarrow$ maximum number of characters in the string including '\0'

Example:

char class[15] ;

the declares class as a string variable having maximum of 15 character including last character '\0'.

3.6.2 INITIALIZING STRING VARIABLE:

Character array can be initialized as that of integer or floating point arrays.

Syntax:

static   dataype variable_name[size]= string ;

Example:

static char state[15] = " TAMIL NADU";

This declares state as a string variable having 15 characters and is stored as shown below.

S [0]	S [1]	S [2]	S [3]	S [4]	S [5]	S [6]	S [7]	S [8]	S [9]	S [10]	S [11]
T	A	M	I	L		N	A	D	U	\0	\0

3.6.3 READING STRINGS:

strings can be read into the memory by means of any one functions namely

> 1) scanf
> 2) getchar
> 3) gets

scanf function:

scanf function with the format specification %s is used to read a string of characters. The most familiar input function **scanf** function.

Syntax:

> **scanf ("%s",variable_name);**

where   variable_name $\Longrightarrow$ valid variable name

the problem with scanf function is the reading stops when it finds a white space character in the input string.

A white space includes blanks, tabs, carriage returns, form feeds, and w lines.

Example:

> char name[15];
> scanf ("%s", name);

Example:

Write a C program to illustrate how to read string from terminal.

```
#include <stdio.h>

int main(){
    char name[20];
    printf("Enter name: ");
    scanf("%s",name);
    printf("Your name is %s.",name);
    return 0;
```

}

Input string → "Dennis Ritchie"

[0]	[1]	[2]	[3]	[4]	[5]	[6]	[7]	[8]	[9]	[10]	[11]	[12]	[13]	[14]
D	e	n	n	i	s	\0	?	?	?	?	?	?	?	?

Output
Enter name: Dennis Ritchie
Your name is Dennis.

Here, program will ignore Ritchie because, **scanf()** function takes only string before the white space.

GETCHAR FUNCTION
the function is used to read a string chracter.

Syntax: **variable_name = getchar ( );**

this function repeatedly string of characters can be read into the memory. The reading is terminated when a new line character '\n' is entered.
Note: that the getchar function has no parameters.

Example:
```
#include <stdio.h>
int main(){
    char name[30],ch;
    int i=0;
    printf("Enter name: ");
    while(ch!='\n')   // terminates if user hit enter
    {
        ch=getchar();
```

```
        name[i]=ch;

        i++;

    }

    name[i]='\0';      // inserting null character at end

    printf("Name: %s",name);

    return 0;

}
```

GETS FUNCTIONS:

This function is used to read a string of text containing characters until a new line character(whitespaces) '\n' is entered. The library function gets available in the <stdio.h> header file.

Syntax: gets (variable_name);

Example:

```
        char str[10];
        Gets(str);
        Printf(" % s " , str );

        [OR ]

        char str[40];
        gets( :"%s",gets(str));
```
Input: "SIVA"
Output:

S	I	V	A	\0	?	?	?	?	?

Example:

```
        int main(){
        char str[30];
        printf("Enter string: ");
        gets(str);    //Function to read string from user.
```

```
printf("string: ");

puts(str);   //Function to display string.

return 0;

}
```

Input :   "Raj kumar"
Output:

R	A	J		K	U	M	A	R	\0

3.6.4 WRITING STRING:

Strings can be displayed on the terminal by means of any one functions namely
2.1.1   prinf
2.1.2   putchar
2.1.3   puts

printf function:

prinf function with format specification %s is used to display strings on the terminal.

Syntax:

Printf(" %s ", variable_name) ;

Where
variable_name   ⟹   array name or string .

We can also specify the precision with which the array is displayed. For instance, the specification.

Example:

#include<stdio.h>

Void main

{

char str[15] = " dennis ritchie

```
printf("%s\n", str);
printf(" %15.6s ", str);
printf(" %15.9s", str);
}
```

Output:

dennis ritchie
dennis
dennis rit

putchar function:

like getchar() function , there is analogous function putchar for writing characters one at a time to the terminal. It takes the form as shown below

Syntax: **putchar(variable_name);**

Example:

```
#include<stdio.h>
Int main()
{
Char str[10];
Printf("Enter a string or character\n");
s=getchar();
str[10] =s;
printf("given string or character is: ");
putchar(str);
return 0;
}
```

Output:

Enter a string or character
program
piven string or character is: program

puts function:

pts function is a function which is used to display string on the terminal.

Example:

```
#include<stdio.h>
Void main()
{
char str[] = " PROGRAMMING IN C\n";
Puts(str);
Puts("programming in c");
}
```

Output:

PROGRAMMING IN C

Programming in c

3.7 STRING HANDLING FUNCTIONS:

C library has a number of string handing function to carry out string manipulations. these functions are defined in the header file <string.h>. the most commonly used string handling functions.

String 1=	0	1	2	3	4	5	6	7	8	9	0	1	2
	V	E	R	Y		\0							

String 2 =	0	1	2	3	4	5
	G	O	O	D	\0	

String 3=	0	1	2	3	4	5
	B	A	D	\0		

3.7.1 C – strcat() function:

strcat( ) function in C language concatenates two given strings. It concatenates source string at the end of destination string.

Syntax: **strcat (destination string , source string) ;**

When this function is executed the contents of the string 2 is joined with string 1 and the character '/0' is placed at the end of the new string string1. String2 remains unchanged. The size of string1 should have enough space to keep the new string.

Example:

The result is

0	1	2	3	4	5	6	7	8	9	0	1	2
V	E	R	Y		G	O	O	D	\0			

Program:

```
#include <stdio.h>
#include <string.h>

int main( )
{
    char source[ ] = " fresh2refresh" ;
    char target[ ]= " C tutorial" ;

    printf ( "\nSource string = %s", source ) ;
    printf ( "\nTarget string = %s", target ) ;

    strcat ( target, source ) ;

    printf ( "\nTarget string after strcat( ) = %s", target ) ;
}
```

OUTPUT:

```
Source string              = fresh2refresh
Target string              = C tutorial
Target string after strcat( ) = C tutorial fresh2refresh
```

3.7.2 Strcpy() function:

This function is used to copy the content of one string into another string. The function strcpy() works like a string assignment operator.

Syntax: **strcpy (string 1, string 2);**
Where string 2= character array name or string constant.

When this function is exected the contents of string 2 is copied into string 1. String 2 remains unchanged. The size of string 1 should have enough space to receive the contents of string 2.

String 1 =

0	1	2	3	4	5
G	O	O	D	\0	

String 2 =

0	1	2	3	4	5

Result
string 1 =

0	1	2	3	4	5
G	O	O	D	\0	

String 2

0	1	2	3	4	5
G	O	O	D	\0	

Example:

```
#include <stdio.h>
#include <string.h>
int main( )
{
char source[ ] = "fresh2refresh" ;
char target[20]= "" ;
printf ( "\nsource string = %s", source ) ;
```

```
printf ( "\ntarget string = %s", target ) ;

strcpy ( target, source ) ;

printf ( "\ntarget string after strcpy( ) = %s", target ) ;

return 0;

}
```

OUTPUT:

> source string = fresh2refresh
> target string = target string after strcpy( ) = fresh2refresh

3.7.3 Strcmp ( ) function:

This strcmp ( ) fuction is used to compare two strings identified by the arguments and have a value 0 if they are equal. If they are not, it have the numeric difference between the first no matching characters in the strings.

Syntax: **strcmp (string 1 , string 2);**

Note:

Returns 0 $\Longrightarrow$ if str1 is same as str2.
Returns <0 $\Longrightarrow$ if strl < str2.
Returns >0 $\Longrightarrow$ if str1 > str2

Example:

```
#include <stdio.h>
#include <string.h>
int main( )
{
  char str1[ ] = "fresh" ;
  char str2[ ] = "refresh" ;
  int i, j, k ;
  i = strcmp ( str1, "fresh" ) ;
  j = strcmp ( str1, str2 ) ;
  k = strcmp ( str1, "f" ) ;
```

```
printf ( "\n %d %d %d", i, j, k ) ;
return 0;
}
```

OUTPUT:

```
0 -1 1
```

3.7.4 Strlen ( ) function:

This function is used to find out the number of characters in the given string.

Syntax: **n= strlen (string);**

Where   n ⟹ is an integer variable which receives the length of the given string.

String ⟹ character array name or string variable or constant.

3.7.5 Strrev ( ) function :

This function is used to reverse a string. strrev( ) function is non standard function which may not available in standard library in C.

Syntax: **n = strrev (string) ;**

Where   n   ⟹   string variable to hold the reversed string.

String   ⟹   string variable or constant, which contains the string to be reversed.

Example:

```
#include<stdio.h>
#include<string.h>

int main()
{
  char str[15] = "Hello";

  printf("String before strrev( ) : %s\n",str);
```

```
        printf("String after strrev( ) : %s", strrev(str));

        return 0;
    }
```

Output :

String before strrev( ) : Hello
String after strrev( )   : olleH

3.7.6 strupr ( ) function :

This strupr ( ) function is used to convert a string in lower case to upper case.

Syntax: **n=strupr (string) ;**

Where   n   ⇒ string variable to hold the converted uppercase string.

String   ⇒ string variable or constant, which contains the lower case string.

Example :

```
            #include<stdio.h>
            #include<string.h>
             int main()
            {
                char str[ ] = "Modify This String To Upper";
                printf("%s\n", strupr(str));
                return  0;
            }
```

Output:

MODIFY THIS STRING TO UPPER

3.7.7 strlwr( ) function:

This strlwr ( ) function is used to convert a string in uppercase to lower case.

Syntax: **n= strlwr(string) ;**

Where   n ⟹ string variable to hold the converted lower case string.

    String   ⟹string variable or constant, which contains the uppercase string.

Example:

```
#include<stdio.h>
#include<string.h>
int main()
{
    char str[ ] = "MODIFY This String To LOwer";
    printf("%s\n",strlwr (str));
    return  0;
}
```

Output: modify this string to lower

3.7.8 Other string function:

String fuction	Syntax	Description	example
strncat ( )	Strncat(s1, s2, n);	Appends a portion of string to another	strncat (str2, str1, 3); – First 3 characters of str1 is concatenated at the end of str2.
strncpy ( )	Strncpy (s1, s2, 5);	Copies given number of characters of one string to another	strncpy (str1, str2, 4) – It copies first 4 characters of str2 into str1.

strstr ( )	Strstr (s1 , s2);	Returns pointer to first occurrence of str2 in str1	Strstr searches the string s1 to see whether the string s2 is contained in s1. If YES return position otherwise, it returns a NULL
C – strchr( )	Strchr(s1, 'single char');	Returns pointer to first occurrence of char in str1	strchr (string,'i');

3.8 Table of strings:

Table of strings means lists of character strings, such as a list of the name of the employees in a department ,list of the name of companies in a cooperate. List of places, etc. this can be represented as a two dimensional array of characters. Each row of the table represents a separate string.

Syntax:

> **char variable_name [row size] [column size];**

Where   char   ⇒   data type
                    variable_name ⇒   variable name
                    row size   ⇒   number of entries in the list or table
                    Column size   ⇒   maximum number of characters in each row.

Example:

Char name[ ][ ] ={"RAJ","JOSEPH","JESTIN","SUDHAKAR","SIVA"};

R	A	J					
J	O	S	E	P	H		
J	E	S	T	I	N		
S	U	D	H	A	K	A	R
S	I	V	A				

FUNCTION

4.1 INTRODUCTION:

A function is a block of code that performs a specific task. Function is classified as one of the derived data types in c. There are two type of functions in c. they are

1) Library Function
2) User Defined Function

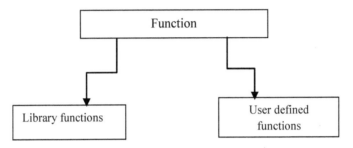

Library functions:

Which are not required to be written by the programmer. But these are available in separate files and the programmer has to include it in the appropriate places. Function prototype and data definitions of these functions are written in their respective header file.

Example:

<strdio.h> header file printf , scanf , etc

If you want to use **printf()**, function, the header file **<stdio.h>** should be included.

A list of the most common libraries and a brief description of the most useful function they contain follows.

1) <Stdio.h> ⟹ Input Output Function
2) <string.h> ⟹ String Functions
3) <math.h> ⟹ Mathematics Functions
4) <stdlib.h> ⟹ Miscellaneous Functions

User defined functions:

Function functions which are defined by the user at the time of writing program. Functions are made for code reusability and for saving time and space.

One or more functions out of this one function should be main in the all c programs. When the c compiler is compile the program main function only exestuation begins. All other functions will be controlled by the function main.

4.2 FUNCTION PROTOTYPE OR DECLARATION:

The variable and an array, a function must also be declared before its called. A function declaration tells the compiler about a function name and how to call the function. The actual body of the function can be defined separately.

Syntax:

> **Function _type function_name(list of arguments);**

This is very similar to the function header line except the terminating semicolon.
- ✓ The parameter or list of argument list must be separated by commas.
- ✓ The parameter names do not need to be the same in the prototype declaration and the function definition.
- ✓ Use of parameter name in the declaration is optional.
- ✓ If the function has no formal parameters, the list is written as (void).

Example:
1) int addNumbers(int a, int b);   // function prototype

Parameter names are not important in function declaration only their type is required, so the following is also a valid declaration
2) int addNumbers (int, int);

FUNCTION DEFINITION:

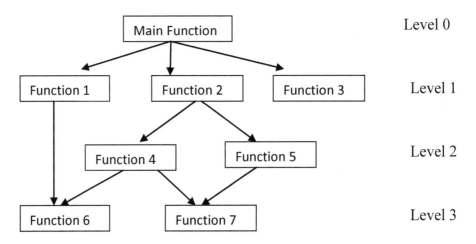

4.3 PART OF USER – DEFINED FUNCTION:

A function that is declare, calling and define by the user is called user define function. Every user define function has three parts as

1) Function Definition.
2) Function Call
3) Function Declaration.

Definition of functions:

Function definition also known as function implementation. A function should be defined before it is used. A function has two parts

1) Function Header
2) Function Body

Syntax:

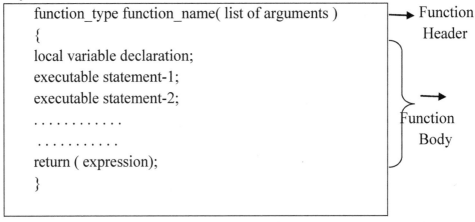

Where

function _type ⟹ Represents the data type of the value returned by the function. if the return type is not explicitly specified, c will assume that it is an void type.

function_name ⟹ valid c identifier and therefore must follow the same rules of formation as other variable name.

List of arguments ⟹ the variables that will receive the data sent by the calling program.

Local variable
declaration ⟹ declaration and statements necessary for performing the required task. The body enclosed in braces.

return ⟹ returns the value evaluated by the function.

Rules:

1. function header should not terminate with semicolon.
2. List of arguments and argument declaration are optional.
3. If the function has no list of arguments and empty parentheses is a must.
4. The expression in the return statement is optional.
5. The parentheses around the expression in the return statement is optional.

Example:

```
#include <stdio.h>
int addNumbers(int a, int b);      // function prototype
int main()
{
    int n1,n2,sum;
    printf("Enters two numbers: ");
```

```
    scanf("%d %d",&n1,&n2);
    sum = addNumbers(n1, n2);      // function call
    printf("sum = %d",sum);
    return 0;

}
int addNumbers(int a,int b)      // function definition

{

    int result;
    result = a+b;
    return result;                // return statement

}
```

4.4 FUNCTION RETURNING NOTHING:

If the function is not to return any value, we can declare the function of type void, which tells c not save any temporary space for a value to be sent by the function.

Syntax:
Void function_name(list of arguments)

Example of function:

```
    int factorial(int x)

    {

    int r=1;
    if(x==1) return 1;
    else r=x*factorial(x-1);
    return r;

    }
```

Factorial is the name of the function. It has one formal parameters x. the statement body has another variable of the formal parameters x. the return statement returns the value of r to other function.

4.5 FUNCTION CALLS:

Function can be called by simply using the function name followed by a list of actual arguments or parameters enclosed within parentheses.

Syntax:

function_name (list of arguments);

Where

Function_name $\Longrightarrow$ already defined function name.

List of argument $\Longrightarrow$ The value will send the data though function definition section.

Rules:

1. Function_name should be the name used in the function definition called function.
2. Data type of the arguments should match with the already defined function called function arguments.
3. The called function returns only one value per call.

Example:

```
#include<stdio.h>
int sum(int , int); //Prototype or Declaration
int main()
{
  int x, y, result;
  printf("Enter value of x and y: ");
  scanf("%d %d", &x, &y);
  result=sum(x, y); //calling of function-sum
  printf("Sum of %d + %d = %d", x, y, result);
  return 0;
}
//Definition of function sum
```

```
int sum(int a, int b)
{
  int res;
  res = a + b;
  return ( res );
}
```

Output:

Enter value of x and y:

15

10

Sum of 15 + 10 = 25

Note:

✓ if actual parameters >formal parameters, the extra actual arguments will be discarded.

✓ If the actual parameters < formal parameters, the unmatched formal arguments will be initialized to some garbage.

Advantage of function:

✓ It provides modularity to the program.

✓ Easy code Reusability. You just have to call the function by its name to use it.

✓ In case of large programs with thousands of code lines, debugging and editing becomes easier if you use functions.

4.6 FUNCTIONS CATEGORY:

We have seen different ways of calling function. A Function is depending on whether arguments are present or not and whether a values is returned or not there are four types of functions.

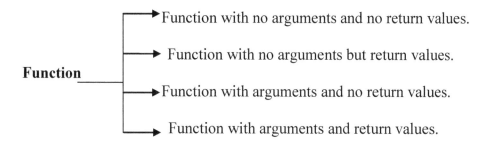

Function
- Function with no arguments and no return values.
- Function with no arguments but return values.
- Function with arguments and no return values.
- Function with arguments and return values.

4.6.1 Function with no arguments and no return values.

This does not receive any arguments (data) from the calling function and does not return any value to the calling function. There is no data transfer between the calling function and the called function.

Syntax:

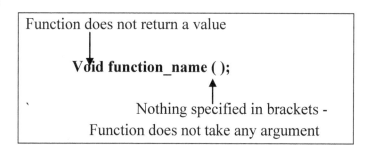

Function does not return a value

Void function_name ( );

Nothing specified in brackets -
Function does not take any argument

Example:

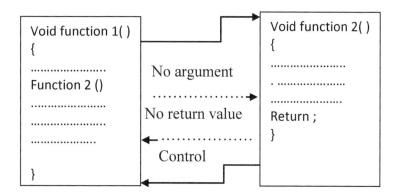

Void function 1( )
{
....
Function 2 ()
....
....
....
}

No argument

No return value

Control

Void function 2( )
{
....
. ...
....
Return ;
}

Program:

```
#include<stdio.h>

void area();  // Prototype Declaration

void main()

{

area();

}

void area()

{

   float area_circle;

   float rad;

   printf("\nEnter the radius : ");

   scanf("%f",&rad);

   area_circle = 3.14 * rad * rad ;

   printf("Area of Circle = %f",area_circle);

}
```

Output:

Enter the radius : 3
Area of Circle = 28.260000

4.6.2 Function with no arguments but return values.

The called Function does not receive any data from the calling Function. It is also a one-way data communication between the calling Function and the called Function.

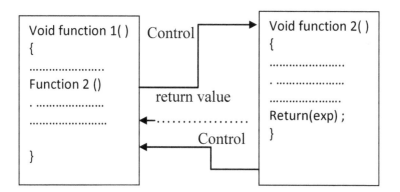

Example:

```
#include<stdio.h>
#include<conio.h>
void main()
{
float sum;
float total();
clrscr();
sum = total();
printf(" Sum = %f\n" , sum);
}
float total()
{
float a, b;
a = 2.0 ;
b = 10.0 ;
return(a+b);
}
```

Output:

sum = 12.000000

4.6.3 Function with arguments and no return values:

✓ Function accepts argument but it does not return a value back to the calling Program.
✓ It is Single (One-way) Type Communication.
✓ Generally Output is printed in the Called function

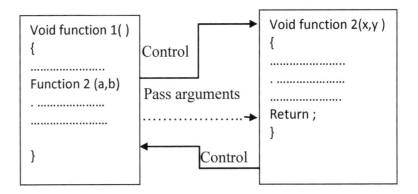

Example:

```
#include<stdio.h>
#include<conio.h>
//------------------------------------------
  void area(float radi);              //Prototype Declaration
//------------------------------------------
void main()
 {
float radi;
  printf("nEnter the radius : ");
  scanf("%f",&radi);
  area(radi);
 getch();
 }
```

```
//----------------------------------------
void area(float radi)
{
float ar;
ar = 3.14 * radi * radi ;
printf("Area of Circle = %f", ar);
}
```

Output:

> Enter the radius : 6
>
> Area of Circle = 113.040000

4.6.4 Function with arguments and one return values:

- ✓ This functions receive arguments(data) from the calling function and return the computed value back to the calling function.
- ✓ It is two ways Communication the arguments pass and result will be receive the calling function.
- ✓

Example:.

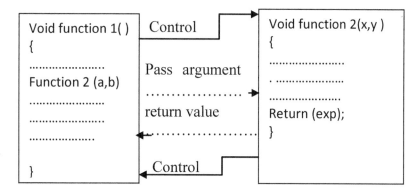

Example:

```
#include <stdio.h>
main()
{
int  i , n , value ;
printf ( "enter the value of n \n " ) ;
scanf ( " % d " , &n ) ;
for ( i = 0 ; i < = n ; i + + )
        {
          value = square ( i ) ;
          printf ( " % d " , i , value ) ;
        }
}
square (m)
int m ;
{
int temp ;
temp = m * m ;
return ( temp ) ;
}
```

Output:

```
Enter n value
4
0 1 4 9 16
```

4.7 RECURSION:

1. A recursion function is one that calls itself again and again.
2. The normal function will be called by other functions by its name. But the recursive function will be called by itself as long as the condition is satisfied.
3. Recursion is a special case of this process.

Syntax:

return_type recursive_func ([argument list])
{
    statements;

    ... ...

    recursive_func ([actual argument]);

    ... ...
}

The general form to represent to flow diagram is

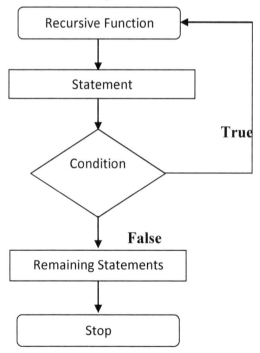

4.7.1 Type of recursion:

1) Direct Recursion
2) Indirect Recursion

Direct Recursion:

A function is said to be direct recursive if it calls itself directly

Function contain without argument

```
void recursion_name( )
{
        ……………….
        …………………..
        recursion_name( ) ;

        …………………
}
int main ( )
{
        …………………………
        recursion_name ( );
        ………………..
}
```

Example:

```
Main( )
{
        Printf(" this is direct recursion function example \n");

        Main( );
// function call itself
}
```

Indirect Recursion :

A function is said to be indirect recursive if it calls another function and this new function calls the first calling function again.

Function contain without argument

int recursion_name 1( )
    {
         ………………
         ……………….
         recursion_name 2( );
         ………………
    }
    int recursion_name2 ( )
    {
         ……………………….
    recursion_name 1 ( ) ;
    }

Example:

The following example calculates the factorial of a given number using a recursive function.

```
#include<stdio.h>
int factorial(int n)
{
   if(n==0)
       return 1;
   else
       return (n * factorial(n-1));
}

int main()
{
   int num,f;
   printf("Enter a number: ");
   scanf("%d",&num);
   f=factorial(num);
```

```
            printf("Factorial of %d = %d",num,f);

            return 0;

      }
```

Explanation:

let us assume num=3.

Since the value of num is not equal to 0 the statement,

Fact=n * factorial(n-1)

1st calling: $\Longrightarrow$ Fact = 3 * factorial (2)

2nd calling: $\Longrightarrow$ Fact= 3 * 2 * factorial (1)

3rd calling $\Longrightarrow$ Fact= 3 * 2 * 1 * factorial (0)

4th calling $\Longrightarrow$ Fact= 3 * 2 * 1 * 1

     Factorial of 3 = 6

4.7.2 Disadvantages of Recursion

✓ Recursive programs are generally slower than non recursive programs because it needs to make a function call so the program must save all its current state and retrieve them again later. This consumes more time making recursive programs slower.

✓ A Recursive program requires more memory to hold intermediate states in a stack. Non recursive programs don't have any intermediate states, hence they don't require any extra memory.

4.8 PASSING ARRAYS TO FUNCTION:

It is also possible to entire array can be passed to a function like variables.

The calling function uses the array name and the size of the array as actual arguments(arguments in the function definition). The called function uses the array name and size of the array as formal arguments(dummy arguments).

Function call

Syntax:

> function_name (array_name, size_of_the_array);

Function definition

Syntax:

> **data_type function_name (array_name, size_of_the_array)**
>
> > **formal argument declaration;**

Rules:
1. The function name in the function call and in function definition should be same.
2. Type of the actual and formal arguments should be same.
3. The array name in the formal argument is declared with empty brackets.
4. The function prototype must show that the argument is an array.

Example:
1) **pass a single element of an array to function**

```
#include <stdio.h>
void display(int a)
  {
  printf("%d",a);
  }
int main(){
  int big[]={6.20.33,14};
  display(big[3]);     //Passing array element c[3] only.
  return 0;
}
```

Output: **14**

2) write a program to arrange n number in ascending order using function:

```
#include < stdio .h >
main( )
{
        int c [ 50 ], n, i ;
        prinf( "enter n numbers n \n " );
        scanf ( " %d " , & n ) ;
        for( i = 0 ; i < n ; i + + )
                scanf ( " % d " , & a [ i ] );
        sort ( c , n );
for ( i = 0; i < n; i + + )
printf( " after sort element  is " ) ;
prinf ( " % d " , a [ i ] ) ;
}
sor ( x, m )
int x [ ] , m ;
{
        int i, j , temp ;
        for ( i = 0 ; i < m – 1 ; i + + )
                for ( j = i + 1 ; j < m  ; j + + )
                        if ( x [ i ] > x [ j ] )
                        {
                                temp = x [ i ] ;
                                x [ i ] = x [ j ];
                                x [ j ] = temp;
                        } }
```

Output:

    Enter n numbers

     53 56 24 63 28 14 36 91

    After sort element is

    14 24 28 36 53 56 63 91

4.9 PASS TWO-DIMENSIONAL ARRAY TO A FUNCTION

      pass two-dimensional array to a function as an argument, starting address of memory area reserved is passed as in one dimensional array

Example:

```
#include <stdio.h>
void display(int array_name[2][2]);
int main()
{
  int array_name[2][2],i,j;
  printf("Enter 4 numbers:\n");
  for(i=0;i<2;++i)
    for(j=0;j<2;++j){
       scanf("%d",&c[i][j]);
    }
  display(array_name);   /* passing multi-dimensional array
to function */
  return 0;
}
void display(int array_name[2][2]){
/* Instead to above line, void display(int array_name[][2]{
is also valid */
  int i,j;
```

```
printf("Displaying:\n");
for(i=0;i<2;++i)
  for(j=0;j<2;++j)
    printf("%d",array_name[i][j]);
}
```

Input: 5 3 15 2

Output: 5   3
                   15   2

4.10 SCOPE OF THE VARIABLES:

✓ Variable is known among the set of functions in a program.
✓ Life time of variable means the period which a variable retains a given value during the execution of the program.
✓ The variable is also known as a identifier, the identifier have a data type, they also have a storage class.
✓ The variable visibility refers to the accessibility of a variable from the memory.

  1) **Automatic variables**
  2) **External variables.**
  3) **Static variables.**
  4) **Register variables.**

Automatic variables or local variable:

The variables declared inside a function are called automatic variables. These are called automatic because, their memory spaces are automatically allocated when the function is called and destroyed automatically when the function is exited. Automatic variables also called private variable because the function variable also declared local or internal variable.

Scope of the automatic variable is it is known only within the function. life time is it is destroyed when we come out of the function.

Syntax:

> **auto data_type variable 1, variable 2, ……………**
> **variable n;**

where

  auto   ⟹ keyword to define automatic variable.
  Data_type   ⟹ valid c data type such as int, float, ect.
  Variable 1 to variable n ⟹ valid identifier name

Structure of local variable:

```
void main ( )
        {
                auto int p=5;           // local variable declaration
and initialization


                …………………

                ++p;                    // call the local variable


                …………………

        }
function1( )
{
float  x = 3.1;                         // local variable declaration
and initialization
float y = 2.0;                          // local variable declaration
and initialization
………………
……………..
x = x + y;                              // call the local variable
…………..
}
```

Example:

```
#include <stdio.h>
Void main ()
{
int p, q;          /* local variable p and q  declaration */
int r;                      /* local variable r declaration*/
p = 10;                     /*  actual initialization to variable  */
q = 20;
r = (p *p) / (q*q)
printf ("value of p= %d, q = %d \n", p, q);
printf(" the result of expression \n r=%d", r);
}
```

Output:

P = 10 q = 20
The result of expression
R = 0.25

Global variables or External variables:

- ✓ The variables which are declared outside the function are called external variables, usually on top of the program.
- ✓ The variable is not declared internally or a specific function, these are common to all the function in the program.
- ✓ The variable are alive and active throughout the program.
- ✓ When the variable definition will automatically allocate storage space.
- ✓ The referred by the variable is same name and same data type.
- ✓ It also called as global variable, because the accessing limited is entire programming.

Syntax:

---

extern data_type variable 1, variable 2, variable 3,……… variable n;

Where

Extern	⇒	key word to define external variable
data_type	⇒	valid c data type such as int, float,.. ect.
Variable 1 to variable n	⇒	valid identifier name

Structure of global variable:

```
extern int p=1 ;              //      global variable    p is
                             declaration  and initialization part
extern float w=2.5;          / * global variable w is declared
                             and  initialization  and  the  data
                             type is also declared   * /
void main ( )
       {
             ++p;
             function1( )
             ………………..
             …………………
```
```
       }
function1( )
{
float  x ;
………………
……………..
x = p + w;                  // call the global variable
…………..
}
```

Example:

```
#include <stdio.h>
void student( void ) ;          // function prototype
int stud_no ;                            // global variable stude_no
is declaration
main()
{
    student() ;                              // function call
    printf( "The students number is %d\n", stud_no ) ;
}
void student( void )                    // function definition
{
    Stud_no = 25 ;
}
```

Output:

The student number is 25

Static variable:

Static variables are variables which retain the values till the end of the program. A variable can be declared static using the keyword static.

Syntax:

static data_type variable 1, variable 2, variable 3,.........variable n ;

The static variable will declared as two type. They are

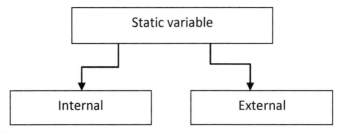

Internal static variables:
- ✓ The variable are declared inside a function, and are accessing limits also within a function.
- ✓ The scope of internal static variables extends up to the end of the function.
- ✓ Static variable are similar to auto (local) variables.

External static variables:
- ✓ An external static variables are variables declared outside the function and are available to all the functions in the program
- ✓ External static variables are available to the functions only within a file.
- ✓ It also act as external (global) variable.

Register variables:
- ✓ Variable also declared inside a function or block
- ✓ The variable should be kept in one of the CPU registers,
- ✓ The variable accessing is much faster than a memory accessing.
- ✓ The variable are stored in the registers are called register variables.
- ✓ Scope of the variable until end of function or block

Syntax:

Register data_type variable

Example:

```
Void main ( )
{
Register int a = 0 ;
Auto int b = 3 ;
Auto char = ' Z ' ;
}
```

STRUCTURES

4.11.1 Introduction:

Array and pointers are powerful tools to represent a group of data items of same dat typed with a single name. But c languageprovides a data type named as structures to do this task. Structures defined as a collection of data items of different types using a single name.

4.11.2 Difference Between Array and Structure

S.no	Array	Structure
1	Array is collection of related data item.	Structure is the collection of deferent data item .
2	Array data are access using index.	Structure elements are access using . operator.
3	Array allocates static memory.	Structures allocate dynamic memory.
4	Array element access takes less time than structures.	Structure elements take more time than Array.
5	Array is a derived data type	Structure is a programmer-defined data type
6	Individual entries in an array are called elements	Structure Individual entries are called members.

4.11.3 Defining a structure:

Structures defined as a collection of data items of different types using a single name. A structure definition contains a keyword struct and a user defined tag field followed by the members of the structure with in braces

Syntax:

```
struct structure_name
{
data_type1  member1;
data_type2  member2;
data_type3  member3;
........................
....................
};
```

Struct   ⟹   keyword to divine structure
Structure_ name ⟹   valid c identifier for name of the structure
data_type   ⟹   valid data type such as int float etc.
member 1 to n   ⟹   different data type of data item or member
                                    function.

RULES:

1. Structure_name is the name given to the structure.
2. Each member declaration should be terminated with semicolon.
3. Structure definition has compound statements, it should have its own opening and closing braces.
4. The structure closing brace is must be terminated with semicolon.

Example:

```
struct employee
    {
    int emp_no = 210 ;
    char name[15] = { " ramkumar " };
    int salary = 20000;
    };
```

The keyword struct declares a structure to hold the details of three data field, namely emp_no, name, and salary. The field of three are members or element of structure variable. Each of the member or structure element is different data type.

4.11.4 Structure variable declaration:

Structure declaration means defining variables to the already defined structure. We can define variables in two way. Don't use member names as variables.

I.   Variable definition along with the structure definition

Syntax:

```
structure structure_name
{
data_type member1;
data_type member2;
.........................
.........................
data_type member n;
};
variable1, variable2, ............, variable n;
```

II.   Variable definition using structure name anywhere in the program.

Syntax:

```
Struct structure_name variable1, variable2, variable;
```

Example:

```
Struct employee
{
Int emp_no;
Char emp_name[15];
Int salary;
};
employee1, employee2, employee3;
```

4.11.5 Typedef structures

the code short and improves readability. In the above discussion we have seen that while using structs every time we have to use the lengthy syntax, which makes the code confusing, lengthy, complex and less readable. The simple solution to this issue is use of typedef. It is like an alias of struct.

Syntax:

```
typedef struct
{
data_type member1;
data_type member2;
....................
.....................
data_type membern;
} variable;
```

4.11.6 Comparison with normal structure and typedef

Code without typedef	Code using tyepdef
struct home_address {	typedef struct home_address{
int local_street;	int local_street;
char *town;	char *town;
char *my_city;	char *my_city;
char *my_country;	char *my_country;
};	}addr;
....	....
....	....
struct home_address var1 = {55, "Dayal bagh", "Agra", "India"};	addr var1 = {55, "Dayal bagh", "Agra", "India"};

4.11.7 Structure initialization:

✓ The members of the structure variable can be assigned initial values at compile time.

✓ The structure should be declared as static type.

Syntax:

static struct structure_name structure_variable = { value1, value2, … value n };

Where

static	$\Longrightarrow$	storage class for structure.
struct	$\Longrightarrow$	keyword to divine structure
structure_ name	$\Longrightarrow$	valid c identifier for name of the structure
Structure_variable	$\Longrightarrow$	member or structure variable declared.
List of values	$\Longrightarrow$	give list of value to initialization for member or structure Variable.

Rules:
1. We cannot initialize individual members inside the structure template.
2. The Order of values enclosed in braces must match the order of members in the structure definition.
3. The uninitialized member will be assigned default values as zero or \0
4. After the list of value must be terminated with semicolon.

Example:

Structure

include <stdio.h>

Struct employee

{

Int emp_no = 210 ;

Char name[15] = { " ramkumar " };

int salary = 20000;

};

int main ( )

{

struct employee emp ;

printf("Emp_name= %d \n emp_name=%s \n emp_salary= %d \n",Emp.emp_no,

emp.name,emp.salary);

}

Output:

Emp_name= 210
emp_name = ramkumar
emp_salary = 2000

4.12 ACCESSING STRUCTURE MEMBERS

✓ Dot operator or member operator '. ' is used to give data to the structure variables individual members.
✓ They should be linked to the structure variable in order to make them meaningful members.
✓ The variable name with a period and the member name are used like any ordinary variable.

Syntax:

Structure_variable . member_name

Example:

Write a c program to assign values to the member of a structure named employee and to display the employe no, name, salary detail.

#include<stdio.h>

struct employee;

{

```
int emp_no;
char emp_name[15];
float salary;
};
Void main( )
{
struct employee detail;
printf("GIVE THE EMPLOYEE DETAILS\n;);
printf("ENTER THE EMPLOYEE NUMBER :");
scanf("Emp_no=%d", & detail.emp_no);
printf("ENTER THE EMPLOYEE NAME :");
scanf("Emp_name=%d", & detail.emp_name();
printf("ENTER THE EMPLOYEE SALARY :");
scanf("Emp_salary=%d", & detail.salary);
printf("Emp_no=%d", detail.emp_no);
printf("Emp_name=%d", detail.emp_name);
printf("Emp_salary=%d", detail.salary);
}
```

Input:
GIVE THE EMPLOYEE DETAILS
ENTER THE EMPLOYEE NUMBER
1024
ENTER THE EMPLOYEE NAME
RAJ
ENTER THE EMPLOYEE SALARY
40000
OUTPUT:

Emp_no	=	1024
Emp_name	=	RAJ
Emp_salary	=	4000

4.13 COPING AND COMPARING STRUCTURE VARIABLES:

the structure variable can be copied into another of the same type, it's possible in c structure using member access operator and assignment operator.

The member accessing operator to access the previous structure variable value is coping and then assignment operator is assign structure value to left side of another member variable.

Syntax:

> **structure_variable2 = structure_variable1**

Structure_variable1 contend is copied there after assigned to structure_variable2.

Example:

```
struct employee
{
int no;
char name [20];
int salary;
};
void main( )
{
int x;
struct employee emp1 = { 9203,"jeo",25000);
struct employee emp2 = { 9321,"mark",15000);
struct employee emp3;
emp3 = emp1 ;
x  =( (emp3.salaray  ==  emp1.salary)&&  (emp3.name  ==
emp1.name) ) ? 1: 0 ;
printf("The employee 1 details\n");
```

printf("%d %s %d\n", emp1.no,emp1.name,emp1.salary);

if(x = 1)

{

printf("The structure variable3 is copied from structure variable1\n");

printf("The employee 3 details");

printf("%d %s %d\n", emp3.no,emp3.name,emp3.salary);

else

printf(" the structure variable in not copied");

}

Output:

The employee 1 details

9203   jeo   25000

The structure variable3 is copied from structure variable1

The employee 3 details

9203   jeo   25000

4.14 ARRYAS OF STRUCTURES:

Array of structures are defined as a group of data item of different data types stored on a consecutive memory location with a common variable name collection an array of structures.

The declare an array of structures, each element of the array representing a structure variable.

Syntax:

> **struct structure_name structure_variable[size] ;**

Structure_variable   ⟹ array name

size   ⟹ no of elements in the array.

Example:

Struct class student[3];

the declaration describe information about two student namely student1 and student2.

Student1[0]	Student2[1]	Student3[2]

This is only one member variable and three student information to allotted the memory The memory allocation is to create three variable space and store three student information.

Suppose the member variable have two or three field, that time to help the accessing member variable operator '.' (dot).

Struct student
{
Char name[15];
Int age;
};
Stuct student stud_bio[3];

4.15 MEMORY ALLOCATION STRUCTURE FORMAT:

S_bio[0]		S_bio[1]		S_bio[2]		Array index no
s_bio 0 [0]	s_bio 0 [1]	s_bio1 [0]	s_bio1 [1]	s_bio 2 [0]	s_bio 2 [1]	Array element index no
						Element

Suppose if we want to describe information about 100 or 1000 students, it is highly difficult to name 1000 different variable. But with the help of the facility available C language these 1000 students (variables) can be called as an array structures. A single name is given to all the 1000 students information contain a single array name.

Example:

Struct student

{

Int stud_no;

Char stud_name[20];

Int percentage;

};

Int main ( )

{

Struct   student   information[4]   =   {{1001,"Daniel", 90},{1002."joseph",70},{1003,"sharma",60},{1004,"mark",91}};

For(i=0;i<4;i++);

{

Print("%d,%s,%d \n", information.

}

}

4.16 Nested structures:

Nesting structures means structures within a structure. When a structure is declared as a member of another structure then it is called structure within structure or nested structure.

Syntax:

```
structure structure_name
{
data_type member1;
........................
data_type membern;
        structure structure_name
            {
```

data_type member1;
data_type member2;
....
....
data_type membern;
} ;
variable1, ... , variablen;
} ;
variable1,   variable2, ...,
variablen;

General format to represent nested structure:

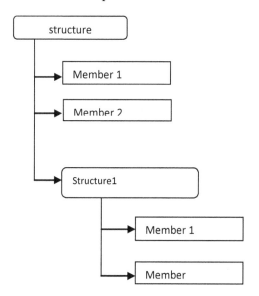

Example:

struct student_information

{

char name[30];

int age;

// inner structure definition

struct stud_address

{

```
        char locality[30];
        char city[20];
        int pincode;
        }address;
    }student;
```

The outer structure struct student_information have three member namely name, and structure address. The inner structure struct stud_address gives the information about student address detail, and the member variable of the inner structure having 3 member namely locality, city and pin code.

4.17 Structures and function:

We can pass the entire structure values as actual argument to functions. there are various methods by which the values of a structure can be transferred from one function to another.

1) Actual argument of the function **Calling function**
2) Entire structure to the **called function**

Calling function:
✓ The actual arguments are then treated independently like ordinary variables.
✓ This is the most elementary method and becomes unmanageable and inefficient when the structure size is large.

Syntax:

function_name (structure_variable_name);

where

function name $\implies$ name of the called function

structure _variable_name$\implies$ actual argument variable name of the defined structure.

Called function:

- ✓ The method involves passing of a copy of the entire structure to the called function.
- ✓ The function is working on a copy of the structure, any changes to structure members within the function are not reflected in the original structure
- ✓ Necessary for the function to return the entire structure back to the calling function.

Syntax:

```
data_type function_name(variable_name)
struct  structure_name variable_name;
{
    ………………..
    …………………..
return(expression);
}
```

Example:

Write a program to pass address of structure variable to user defined function and display the contents.

```
#include<stdio.h>
#include<conio.h>
struct book
{
char name[28];
char author[30];
int pages;
};
void main()
{
struct book b1 = { " PROBLEM SOLVING USING C","R. SIVARAJ",982};
show(&b1);
}
```

```
show (struct book *b2)
{
clrscr ();
printf("\n %s by %s of %d page", b2->name,b2->author,b2->pages.);
}
```

Output:

PROBLEM SOLVING USNG C by R.SIVARAJ of 982 pages.

4.18 UNIONS

 ✓ Union is like a structure data type in which all the members share the same memory area.
 ✓ In the structure each member has its own memory location whereas, members of unions have same memory location.
 ✓ The compiler allocates a memory space that is large enough to store the largest variable type in the union.

Syntax:

```
Union union_tag_field
{
Data_type member1;
Data_type member2;
.................
    Data_type member;
} variable1,variable2,..... variable;
```

where

union	⟹	keyword to define union
union_tag_field	⟹	name of the union – valid name
member1 to member n	⟹	different data type of data item or member function.

Example:

> **union** item
>
> {
>
> int m;
>
> float x;
>
> char c;
>
> }It1;

Explanation:

This declares a variable **It1** of type union **item**. This **union** contains three members each with a different data type. However only one of them can be used at a time. This is due to the fact that only one location is allocated for a **union** variable, irrespective of its size. The compiler allocates the storage that is large enough to hold largest variable type in the **union**. In the **union** declared above the member **x** requires 4 bytes which is largest among the members in 16-bit machine. Other members of **union** will share the same address.

Uses of unions:

✓ Unions conserve memory space.
✓ They are useful for applications involving number of variables, where values need not be assigned to all elements at one time.

4.18.1 Difference between unions and structures:

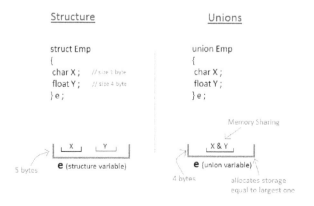

Structure	C Union
Structure allocates storage space for all its members separately.	Union allocates one common storage space for all its members. Union finds that which of its member needs high storage space over other members and allocates that much space
Structure occupies higher memory space.	Union occupies lower memory space over structure.
The address of each member will be in ascending order This indicates that memory for each member will start at different offset values.	The address is same for all the members of a union. This indicates that every member begins at the same offset value.
Altering the value of a member will not affect other members of the structure.	Altering the value of any of the member will alter other member values.

Structure example:
struct student {
int mark;
char name[6];
double average;
};
	Union example:
	union student {
	int mark;
	char name[6];
	double average;
	};

For above structure, memory allocation will be like below. int mark – 2B char name[6] – 6B double average – 8B Total memory allocation = 2+6+8 = 16 Bytes	For above union, only 8 bytes of memory will be allocated since double data type will occupy maximum space of memory over other data types. Total memory allocation = 8 Bytes

Program:

```
#include<stdio.h>
#include<conio.h>
void main ( )
{
union result
{
int marks;
{
int marks;
char grade;
};
struct res
{
char name[20];
int age;
union result perf;
};
data;
clrscr( );
printf("size of union:%d\n",sizeof(data.perf));
printf("size of structure:%d\n",sizeof(data));
}
```

Output:

Size of union: 2

Size of structure: 19

POINTERS AND FILE MANAGEMENT

5.1 INTRODUCTION TO POINTERS:

The variables are used to hold data values during the execution of a program. every variable when declared occupy certain memory location. In c it is possible to access and display the address of the memory location of variable using & operator with variable name. The pointer variable is needed to store the memory address of any variable. The pointer is denoted by (*) asterisk symbol.

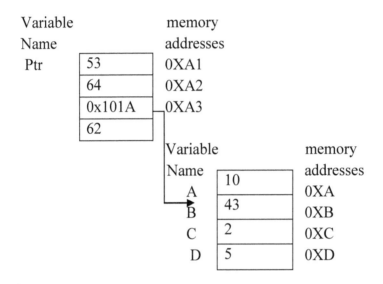

The variable that holds memory address is called **pointer variables**. A **pointer** variable is therefore nothing but a variable that contains an address, which is a location of another variable. Value of **pointer variable** will be stored in another memory location.

5.2 FEATURES OF POINTERS:

✓ Pointer increases the execution speed of the program.
✓ Pointers save the memory space.
✓ Pointers reduce the length and complexity of a program.
✓ Pointers enable us to access a variable that is defined outside the function.

✓ Pointers are used to pass information back and forth between a function and its reference point.
✓ Pointers are used with data structures. They are useful for representing two-dimensional and multi-dimensional arrays.

5.3 POINTER VARIABLES DECLARATION:

A pointer is a memory variable that stores a memory address. Pointer can have any name that is legal for other variable and it is declared in the same fashion like other variables but it is always denoted by "* "operator. Pointer variables must be declared before it is used in the program like other variables.

Syntax:

> **data_type *pointer_variable_name ;**

where

        data_type   ⇨ Type of the variable pointed by pointer variable such as int, float, etc.

        *   ⇨ To identify the variable as pointer

pointer_variable_nam ⇨ Valid variable name or identifier name, to point to an data.

Rules:
1. Pointer variables should be a valid variable name.
2. Asterisk (*) is not the part of the variable name but it is to denote the type of the variable as pointer.
3. Data type refers to the type of the variable pointer by the pointer variable.
4. Initially the pointer does not point to anything byt the programmer must assign it a value.

Example:

    Int *p;   // integer pointer

    Float *q

Declares the variable p as a pointer variable that points to an integer data type and another pointer variable q is to points to an float type of data..

5.4 INITIALIZATION OF POINTER VARIABLES:

✓ The process of assigning the address of a variable to a pointer variable is known as initialization. The address of the variables can be got with the help of the address operator "&".

✓ The operator "&" immediately preceding a variable returns the address of the variables associated with it.

✓ Once a pointer variable has been declared we can use the assignment operator to initialize the variable.

Syntax:

> data_type pointer_variable = & variable;

Example:

```
int a = 10 ;
int *ptr ;        //pointer declaration
ptr = &a ;        //pointer initialization
[or]
int *ptr = &a ;   //initialization and declaration together
```

the memory address of the variable a is assigned to the pointer variable *ptr. If 20 is the address of the variable a. ptr got the value 20.

Program:

```
#include<stdio.h>
void main ( )
{
int a;
int *b;
a = 50;
b = &a;
printf(" the content of the pointer b= %d \n",*b);
printf("the address of the pointer b= %d \n", b);
}
```

Output:

> The content of the pointer b=50;
> The address of the pointer b= 25363

5.5 POINTER ARITHMETIC:

Pointer arithmetic is very important to understand, if you want to have complete knowledge of pointer. Increase, decease, prefix, & postfix operations can be performed with the help of the pointers. In this topic we will study how the memory addresses change when you increment a pointer. But in this case to use arithmetic operator have some memory size need to store the variable, it depend open the system. Suppose the machine has 16 bit process operation.

Pointer and arithmetic operation:

Type	Size(bytes)
int or signed int	2
char	1
long	4
float	4
double	8
long double	10

Data type	Initial address	operation		Address after operations		Required bytes
Int a=2	2004	++	--	2006	2002	2
char c= 's'	2421	++	--	2422	2420	1
Float f=5.3	2556	++	--	2560	2552	4

Example:

Write a program to perform different arithmetic operations using pointers.

```
#include<stdio.h>
#include<conio.h>
        Void main ( )
        {
        Int a=20, b=10, *p, *q;
        P = &a;
        Q=&b;
        Clrscr( );
        prinrf("\n addition a+b =%d",*p+b);
        prinrf("\n subtraction a-b =%d",*p-b);
        prinrf("\n division a/b =%d",*p/*q);
        }
```

Output:

        Addition a + b =30
        Subtraction a-b = 10
        Division a/b= 2

5.6 POINTERS AND ARRAYS:

An array name can be defined as a constant pointer that points to the address of the first element in the array. The elements of the array together with their addresses can be displayed by using array name itself. Array elements are always stored in contiguous memory locations. Consider the array declaration.

Syntax:

> **data _type array_name[pointer_address][size]**

Example:
        int arr[4] = { 3,6,8,10 };

Assuming that the base address of **arr** is 100 and each integer requires two byte, the five element will be stored as follows

Element	arr[0]	arr[1]	arr[2]	arr[3]
value	3	6	8	10
Address	100	102	104	106

Here variable arr will give the base address, which is a constant pointer pointing to the element, arr[0]. Therefore arr is containing the address of arr[0] i.e 1000.

arr is equal to &arr[0]   // by default

We can declare a pointer of type int to point to the array arr.

int *p;

p = arr;

or p = &arr[0]; //both the statements are equivalent.

Program:

```
#include<stdio.h>
void main( )
{
static int a[5] ={ 30,100,50,20,90};
int *p;
int i;
p=&a[0];
printf("contents of the arra \n");
for(i=0;i<5;i++)
printf("%d \n ", *(p+1));
}
```

Output:

30
100
50
20
90

5.7 POINTERS AND TWO DIMENSIONAL ARRAYS:

In one dimensional array we saw that the address of the first element is assigned to the pointer variable like that in two dimensional array also the address of the zeroth row and zeroth column are assigned to the pointer variable.

> **int arr[2][2] ={ {15,30},{50,20} };**
> **int *x;**
> **X=&a[0][0];**

0	1	
15	30	0X
50	20	1X+1

EXAMPLE:

Write a program to display array elements and their address using pointers.

```
#include<stdio.h>
void mani( )
{
int i,j=1, *r;
int a[2][2] ={ {6,9},{8,9} );
clrscr();
print("elements of an array with their address\n");
r=&a[0][0];
for(i=0;i<4;i++,j++)
{printf("%5d[%5u]",*®,r);
r++;
if(j=2);
j=0;
}
}
```

}

OUTPUT:

Elements of an array with their address.

6 [2002]   9 [2004]

8 [2006]   9 [2008]

5.8 POINTERS AND CHARACTER STRINGS:

Strings are treated like character arrays and therefore, the are declared and initialized as follows. String is an array of characters terminated by null character '\0'. We can represent strings using pointer.

Syntax:

> **data_type array_name[size] = { };**

Example:

Char *str = "welcome"

To create a string for the literal and then stores its address in the pointer variable str

The pinter str now points to the first character of the string "welcome"

Program:

Write a program to read string from keyboard and display it using character pointer.

```
#include<stdio.h>

void main ( )

{

char name[15],*ch;

printf("enter your name:");

gets(name);
```

```
ch=name;
// store base address of string name
while(*ch!='\0')
{
printf("%c",*ch);
ch++;
}
}
```

Output:

Enter your name: suresh
suresh

5.9 POINTERS TO FUNCTIONS:

A function, like a variable, has a type and an address location in the memory it is therefore, possible to declare a pointer to a function, which can then be used as an argument in another function.

syntax:

data_type (* function_pointer_name)( );

Where

* function_pointer_name ⟹ pointer to a function name

5.9.1 Pointer as function argument

We pass addresses to a function, the parameters receiving the addresses should be pointers. The process of calling a function using pointers to pass the addresses of variable is known as call by reference

```
#include<stdio.h>
Int main( )
{
Int z;
Z = 100;
Change(&z);
Printf("%d \n", z);
```

```
        }
        Change(int *r)
        {
        *p = *p+200;
        }
```
Output:
```
        300
```

5.9.2 Function returning pointers:

A function can return a single value by its name or return multiple values through pointer parameters. A function can also return a pointer to the calling function. In this case you must be careful, because local variables of function doesn't live outside the function, hence if you return a pointer connected to a local variable, that pointer be will pointing to nothing when function ends.

Example:
```
        #include <stdio.h>
        #include <conio.h>
        int* big(int*, int*);
        void main()
        {
        int p=15;
        int q=92;
        int *z;
        z=big(&p, &q);
        printf("%d The biggest no",*z);
        }
        int* big(int *x, int *y)
        {
        if(*x > *y)
           return x;
```

else

  return y;

}

Output:

  The biggest no 92

5.10 Pointers and structures:
  1. Address of Pointer variable can be obtained using '&' operator.
  2. Address of such Structure can be assigned to the Pointer variable .
  3. Pointer Variable which stores the address of Structure must be declared as Pointer to Structure .

  Syntax:

```
struct structure_name {
    member1;
    member2;

      .

      .
};

int main()
{
    struct structure_name *ptr;
}
```

Example:

```
#include <stdio.h>
#include <string.h>
struct student
{
    int id;
```

```
        char name[25];
        float percentage;
    };
    int main()
    {
        int i;
        struct student record1 = {1, "Raju", 90.5};
        struct student *ptr;
        ptr = &record1;
        printf("Records of STUDENT1: \n");
        printf(" Id is: %d \n", ptr->id);
        printf(" Name is: %s \n", ptr->name);
        printf(" Percentage is: %f \n\n", ptr->percentage);
        return 0;
    }
```

Output:

```
    Records of STUDENT1:
    Id is: 1
    Name is: Raju
    Percentage is: 90.500000
```

FILE:

We used scanf and printf function to read and write data to and from the computers though the console. If computers deal with large amount of data as input (read) and output (output) then both methods are not efficient. The best way is to use files to give data to the computers and get data from the computer.

5.11.1 DEFINITION OF FILE:

File is a set of record that can be accessed through the set of library function. The set of library function is contain a single header file <stdio.h> like printf, scanf etc ,though header file is common input and output library function in file.

Syntax:

File * pointer_variable ;

Where

file   ⟹   defined data type

pointer_variable   ⟹   pointer to the data type file

Example:

    FILE *fp;

The statement declares the variable fp as a "pointer to data type FILE". As the file stated earlier, FILE is a structure that is defined in the I/O library.

5.11.2 STREAMS AND FILE TYPES:

Stream means reading and writing of dat. The streams are designed to allow the user to access the files efficiently

The FILE object contains all the information about stream like current position, pointer to any buffer, error and EOF(end of file).

Type of file:

There are two types of files

    1) **Sequential File**

    2) **Random Access File**

1) Sequential File:

✓ In this type data are kept sequentially. If we want to read the last record of the file we need to read all the records before that record.

✓ It take more time

✓ If we desire to access the 10th record then the first 9 records should be read sequentially for reaching to the 10th record.

2) Random Access File:

✓ In this type data can be read and modified randomly.

✓ In this type if we want to read the last records of the file , we can read it directly

✓ It takes less time as compared to sequential file

5.11.3 FILE OPERATION:

1) Opening of file $\implies$ A fill has to be opened before beginning of read and write operation

2) Reading or writing file $\implies$ File is opened using fopen ( )

3) Closing file. $\implies$ The file that is opened from the fopen( ) should be closed.

File Handling Functions

Function	Operation
fopen( )	Creates a new file for read / write operation
Feof( )	Test the end of file condition
Fclose( )	Closes a file associated with file pointer
READ OPERATION	
fscanf( )	Reads all types of data values from a file.
getw( )	Reads an integer from the file.
Fgetc( )	Reads the character from current pointer position and advances the pointer to next character.
Getc ( )	Same as fgetc ( )

WRITE OPERATION	
putc( )	Writes string to the file.
fprintf( )	Writes all types of data values to the file.
putw ( )	Writes an integer to the file
Random access file	
fseek( )	Sets the pointer position anywhere in the file.
Ftell ( )	Return the current position of the pointer in the given file

1) Opening a file

Opening of file creates a link between the operating system and the file function. we have to specify the name of file and its's mode to the operating system. The important task is carried out by the structure file that is defined in stdio.h header file.

Syntax:

> **FILE *pointer_variable;**
> **Pointer_variable = fopen("file_name","mode");**

Where

pointe_variable $\implies$ variable which contains the address of the type FILE

file_name $\implies$ name of the file.

Mode may be any one of the following

R	$\implies$	open the file for reading only
W	$\implies$	open the file for writing only
A	$\implies$	open the file for appending
R+	$\implies$	open the file for reading and writing
W+	$\implies$	open the file for reading and writing
A+	$\implies$	open the file for reading and appending

Example:

> FILE *fpt
>
> Fpt = fopen("myfiles","r");

The file myfile is opened for reading. If the file does not present an error will occur

Fopen( )performs important tasks:
1) It searches the disk for opening the file.
2) In case the file exists, it loads the file from the disk into memory if the file is found with huge contents then it loads the file part by part.
3) If the file in not existing this function returns a NULL.NULL is a macro defined character in the header file "stdio.h".
4) the indicates that it is unable to open file. There may be following reasons for failure of
   fopen ( ) functions.
   1) When the file is in protected or hidden mode.
   2) The file may be used by another program.
5) It locates a character pointer, which points the first character of the file. Whenever a file is opened the character pointer points to the first character of the file.

Test for end of file:
> Feof () function is used to test the end of file condition.

Syntax:

Feof(pointer_variable)

This function returns a non – zero value if the end of file is reached, else zeo.

Example: num = feof(fp)

2) Close a file:

An opened file must be closed after all operations on it have been completed. His ensures that all outstanding information associated with the file is flushed out from the buffers and all liks to the file are broken.

Syntax:

Fclose(file_pointer_variable) ;

Example:

```
. . . . . . . . . .
. . . . . . . . . .
FILE *fp1,fp2;
Fp1 = fopen("INPUT","w");
Fp2 = fopen("OUTPUT","r");

. . . . . . . . . . . . .
Fclose(fp1);
Fclose(fp2);
```

This program opens two files and closes them after all operations on them are completed once a file is closed its file pointer can be reused for another file

3) READING A FILE

Fscanf ( ) Function:

fscanf ( ) The fscanf function is used to read data items to the file whose pointer is opened in the reading mode. fscanf function performs Input operations on files.

Syntax:

Fscanf(pointe_variable, "control_string",list) ;

Where
pointer_variable ⟹ The pointer which contains the address of the file.
control_string ⟹ The format commands such as %s, %d, %f etc.
list ⟹ list of variable or string to be read from the file.

Example:

> fscanf (fp1, "%s %d", item & quantity);

Where "item"is an array variable of type and quantity is an int variable. Fscanf returns the no. of items when the end of file is reached 'i' returns the value Eof

Program:
Write a program to enter dat into the text file and read the same. Use "w+" file mode use fscanf() to read the contents of the file.

```
#include<stdio.h>
void main( )
{
file *fp;                         //file pointer defining
char text[20];
int age;
fp = fopen ("text.txt","w+");     // open a file operation fopen(
)
clrscr ( );
printf("name \t age \n");
scanf("%s %d",text,&age);
fprintf(fp,"%s %d",text,age);     //write a file operation using
fprintf( )
printf("name \t age \n");
fscanf(fp,"%s %d",text,&age);     // read a file operation
using fscanf( )
printf("%s \t %d \n",text,age);
fclose(fp);                       // file close operation fclose( )
}
```

Output:

        Name age

        Ram   25

Getw ( ) Function:

These functions return the integer value from a file and increase the file pointer. These functions would be useful when we deal with only integer data.

Syntax:

> **Number =getw (file_pointer);**

Where

Number   ⇨   integer value

getw   ⇨   Reads an integer from the file

file_pointer⇨   The pointer which contains the address of the file.

Example:

```
FILE *fp
int  num;
fp=fopen ("input", "r");
while (num=getw(fp)!=EOF)
printf("%d", num);
```

Where read an integer value from the file whose file pointer is fp and assigned the reading numbers to num. The reading is terminated when getw encounters the end of file mark EOF.

Getc ( ) Function:

This function reads a single character from the opened file and moves the file pointer. It returns EOF, if end of file is reached. Getc( ) is used to read a character from a file that has been opened in read mode.

Syntax:

character_variable = getc(file_pointer);

Where

character_variable ⇒ single character variable name like as A, C, R, ect

getc ⇒ reads a single character file function key

Example:

```
file  *fp;
char  c;
fp=fopen ("input", "r");
while(c=getc(fp)!=Eof)        // read a single character
putchar ( c );               // write a single character
```

Program:

```
#include<stdio.h>
#include<process.h>
void main( )
{
file *f;
chara c;
clrscr ( );
f=fopen(" mydata.txt","r");
If(f==NULL)
{
printf("\n cannot open file");
exit(1);
}
```

while(c=getc(f)!=EOF)

pring("%d",c);

fclose(f);

}

Output:

        Akash

        Ram

        Suresh

        Siva

Fgetc ( ) Function:

This function is similar to **getc ( )** function. it also reads a character and increases the file pointer position. If any error or end of file is reached it returns **EOF**.

Syntax:

character_variable = fgetc(file_pointer);

where

character_variable ⟹   single character variable name like as A,C,R,ect

fgetc   ⟹   Reads a character and increases the file pointer position.

Example:

```
file *fp;
char  c;
fp=fopen ("input", "r");
while(c=fgetc(fp)!=Eof)     // read a single character
putchar ( c );              // write a single character
```

Writing a file

Fprintf ( ) Function:

Fprintf ( ) this function is used for writing characters, strings, integers, floats etc. to the file. It contains one more parameter that is file pointer, which points the opened file.

Syntax:

> **Fprintf(pointe_variable, "control_string",list) ;**

Where
pointer_variable $\Longrightarrow$ The pointer which contains the address of the file.
control_string $\Longrightarrow$ The format commands such as %s, %d, %f etc.
list $\Longrightarrow$ list of variable or string to be read from the file.

Example:

fprintf (fp1, "%s %d %f", name age,7.5);

Where 'name is an array variable of type and age is an int variable.

Program:

Write a program to open a myfile and write a some text using fprintf ( ) function. open the file and verify the contents.

```
#include<stdio.h>
#include<conio.h>
void main( )
{
FILE *fp;
char myfile[50];
fp = fopen("myfile.txt","w");
```

```
clrscr ( );
printf("enter text here:");
gets(text);
fprintf(fp,"%s",text);
fclose(fp);
}
```

Output:

Enter text here: have a good day.

Putc ( ) Function:

The function is used to write a single character into a file.if an error occurs it returns EOF.

Syntax:

Putc (character_variable, file_pointer);

character_variable $\implies$ single character variable name like as A,C,R,ect

putc $\implies$ write a single character file function key

Example:

```
FILE *fp;
Char  C;
Fp=fopen("input", "w");
While (c = getchar( c )!= EOF)
Putc(c, fp);                    //write a single character
```

Putw ( ) Function:

The simplest I/O integer oriented function is putw( ). 'putw' is used to create an integer value to a file that has been opened in write mode. The general form statement is

Syntax:

> Putw(num,file_pointer);

Example :

> FILE *fp
>
> Int num;
>
> Fp=fopen ("INPUT", "w");
>
> Scanf("%d", & num);
>
> While (num!= fp)
>
> Putw(num,fp);
>
> Scanf("%d", & num);

Where read a number through to the variable 'num' and put the number into the file whose file pointer is fp. The waiting is terminted when 'Putw' encounters the end of file mark Eof (i.e,num=0)

Fseek ( ) function:

This function is used to move the file pointer to any desired location within the file.

Syntax:

> **Fseek (pointer_variable, offset, position);**

Where

Pointer_variable $\Longrightarrow$ pointer which contains address of the file

Offset $\Longrightarrow$ this gives the number of positions to be moved from the location given in position ot must be a long integer.

position $\Longrightarrow$ it is a integer number

Location of file pointer:.

Integer Values	Constant	Location in the file
0	SEEK_SET	Beginning of the file
1	SEEK_CUR	Current position of the file pointer.
2	SEEK_END	End of the file

Example:

Fseek(fp,10,seek_cur)

Ftell( ) function:

This function is used to return the current position of the pointer in the given file.

Syntax:

N= ftell(pointer_variable);

Where

Ftell $\implies$ keyword to return the current position.

Pointer_variable $\implies$ pointer which contains the address of the file

n $\implies$ numeric variable to receive the position.

The return position is always relative to the beginning of the file and is always a long integer.

Example:

> FILE *ptr;
> Long n;
> ....
> ....
> N=ftell(pt);
> ....

5.11.4 COMMAND LINE ARGUMENTS:

command line arguments are arguments that allow parameters to be passed to main from operating system. There are two arguments namely

1) argc $\implies$ is an integer variable.
2) argv $\implies$ is an array of pointer to characters.

Each string in the array of pointers **argv** represent a parameter that is passed to main and the value of **argc** gives the number of parameters to be passed.

Syntax:

c> program_name string1, string2, ... , string n

Where
program_name $\implies$ name of the executable program wit **.exe**
string1,string2,.... String n $\implies$ list of arguments.

- ✓ When this comman is executed the variable argc automatically counts the number of arguments on the comman line and it takes the value argc=(n+1).
- ✓ The pointer variable argv takes the value of argc i.e. n+1 as its size.
- ✓ The first location argv[0] contains the first parameter program name, the second location contains the strng 1, the third location contains strin 2 and so on.

Argc	=	n+1	
Argv[0]		=	program name
Argv[1]		=	string 1
Argv[2]		=	string 2
………………………..			
………………………..			
Argv[n]		=	string n

Example:

main(argc,argv)

int argc;

char *argv[ ];

…………

…………

Int this argc = 3

Argv[0]	=	prg
Argv[1]	=	file1
Argv[2]	=	file2

Program:

```
#include<stdio.h>
#include<conio.h>
Int Main(int argc,char *argv[ ])
{
Int x;
Clrscr ( );
Printf("\n total number of argument are %d \n",argc);
For (x=0;x<argc;x++)
Printf("%s\t",argv[x]);
Getch( );
```

Return 0;

}

Output:

Total number of arguments are 4

C:\TC\C.EXE A B C

Explanation:

To execute this program one should create its executable file and run it from the command prompt with required arguments. The above program is executed using following steps.

1) Compile the program.
2) Makes its exe file(executable file).
3) Switch to the command prompt. (c:\tc>)
4) Make sure that the exe file is available in the current directory.
5) Type following bold lin

C:\TC>C.EXE HELP ME

Dynamic Memory Allocation

✓ It is a process of allocating or de-allocating the memory at run time it is called as dynamically memory allocation.

✓ When we are working with array or string static memory allocation will be take place that is compile time memory management.

✓ When we ate allocating the memory at compile we cannot extend the memory at run time, if it is not sufficient.

✓ By using compile time memory management we cannot utilize the memory properly

✓ In implementation when we need to utilize the memory more efficiently then go for dynamic memory allocation.

✓ By using dynamic memory allocation whenever we want which type we want or how much we type that time and size and that we much create dynamically.

5.12.1 Dynamic Memory Allocation Functions in C:

Dynamic memory allocation related all predefined functions are declared in following header files.

1. malloc()
2. calloc()
3. realloc()
4. free()

Function	Syntax
malloc ()	malloc (number *sizeof(int));
calloc ()	calloc (number, sizeof(int));
realloc ()	realloc (pointer_name, number * sizeof(int));
free ()	free (pointer_name);

Malloc() Function In C

- ✓ malloc () function is used to allocate space in memory during the execution of the program.
- ✓ malloc () does not initialize the memory allocated during execution. It carries garbage value.
- ✓ malloc () function returns null pointer if it couldn't able to allocate requested amount of memory.

Syntax:

Mem_allocation_variable = malloc (number *sizeof(int));

Program:

```
#include <stdio.h>
#include <string.h>
#include <stdlib.h>
int main()
{
    char *mem_allocation;
                    /* memory is allocated dynamically */
    mem_allocation = malloc( 20 * sizeof(char) );
    if( mem_allocation== NULL )
    {
      printf("Couldn't able to allocate requested memory\n");
    }
    else
    {
      strcpy( mem_allocation,"Dynamically_mem_allocation");
```

```
        }
        printf("Dynamically allocated memory content : " \
             "%s\n", mem_allocation );
        free(mem_allocation);
    }
```

OUTPUT:

```
        Dynamically allocated memory content :
        Dyabanucall_mem_allocation
```

calloc()

- ✓ By using calloc() we can create the memory dynamically at initial stage.
- ✓ calloc() required 2 arguments of type count, size-type.
- ✓ Count will provide number of elements; size-type is data type size.
- ✓ calloc() will creates the memory in blocks format.
- ✓ Initial value of the memory is zero.

Syntax

```
ptr=(cast-type*)calloc(n,element-size);
```

This statement will allocate contiguous space in memory for an array of *n* elements. For example:

$$ptr=(float*)calloc(25,sizeof(float));$$

This statement allocates contiguous space in memory for an array of 25 elements each of size of float, i.e, 4 bytes.

Program:

```c
#include <stdio.h>
#include <string.h>
#include <stdlib.h>
int main()
{
    char *mem_allocation;
    /* memory is allocated dynamically */
    mem_allocation = calloc( 20, sizeof(char) );
    if( mem_allocation== NULL )
    {
        printf("Couldn't able to allocate requested memory\n");
    }
    else
    {
        strcpy( mem_allocation,"fresh2refresh.com");
    }
        printf("Dynamically allocated memory content   : " \
            "%s\n", mem_allocation );
        free(mem_allocation);
}
```

OUTPUT:

> Dynamically allocated memory content :
> fresh2refresh.com

realloc()

✓ By using realloc() we can create the memory dynamically at middle stage.
✓ Generally by using realloc() we can reallocation the memory.
✓ Realloc() required 2 arguments of type void*, size_type.
✓ Void* will indicates previous block base address, size-type is data type size.
✓ Realloc() will creates the memory in bytes format and initial value is garbage.

Syntax

> ptr=realloc(ptr,newsize);

Here, *ptr* is reallocated with size of newsize.

Program:

```
#include <stdio.h>
#include <stdlib.h>
int main(){
    int *ptr,i,n1,n2;
    printf("Enter size of array: ");
```

```
    scanf("%d",&n1);
    ptr=(int*)malloc(n1*sizeof(int));
    printf("Address of previously allocated memory: ");
    for(i=0;i<n1;++i)
        printf("%u\t",ptr+i);
    printf("\nEnter new size of array: ");
    scanf("%d",&n2);
    ptr=realloc(ptr,n2);
    for(i=0;i<n2;++i)
        printf("%u\t",ptr+i);
    return 0;
}
```

free()

✓ When we are working with dynamic memory allocation memory will created in heap area of data segment.
✓ When we are working with dynamic memory allocation related memory it is a permanent memory if we are not de-allocated that's why when we are working with dynamic memory allocation related program, then always recommended to deleted the memory at the end of the program.
✓ By using free(0 dynamic allocation memory can be de-allocated.
✓ free() requires one arguments of type void*.
✓ By using malloc(), calloc(), realloc() we can create maximum of 64kb data only.
✓ In implementation when we need to create more than 64kb data then go for formalloc(), forcalloc() and forrealloc().

✓ By using free() we can de-allocate 64kb data only, if we need to de-allocate more than 64kb data then go for

Syntax

> free(ptr);

This statement cause the space in memory pointer by ptr to be deallocated.

Examples of calloc() and malloc()

Write a C program to find sum of n elements entered by user. To perform this program, allocate memory dynamically using malloc() function.

```
#include <stdio.h>
#include <stdlib.h>
int main(){
    int n,i,*ptr,sum=0;
    printf("Enter number of elements: ");
    scanf("%d",&n);
    ptr=(int*)malloc(n*sizeof(int));   //memory allocated
using malloc
    if(ptr==NULL)
    {
        printf("Error! memory not allocated.");
        exit(0);
    }
    printf("Enter elements of array: ");
    for(i=0;i<n;++i)
```

```
    {
        scanf("%d",ptr+i);
        sum+=*(ptr+i);
    }
    printf("Sum=%d",sum);
    free(ptr);
    return 0;
}
```

Bibliography:

Ashok N. Kamthane., Programming With ANSI and Turbo C, Dorling Kindersley(india) Pvt. Ltd, 2006.

Barkakati, N., Microsoft C Bible, SAMS,1990

Brian W. Kernighan., The C Programmin Language Second Edition, Prentice Hall, Englewood Cliffs, New Jerse, 1988

Barker, L., C Tools for Scientists and Engineers, McGraw-hill,1989.

Berry, R. E. and Meekings; B.A.E., A Book on c, Macmillan, 1987.

Edwin Dayanand. I., Data Structures Using C, N.V.Publication,1999.

Hancock, L. and Krieger, M., The C primer, McGraw-Hill, 1987.

Hunt, W.J., The C Toolbox, Addison - Weslary, 1985.

Hunter,B.H., Understanding C., Sybex, 1985.

Kernighan,B.W. and Ritchie, D.M., The C Programming Language, Prentice-Hall, 1977.

Kochan, S.G., Programming in C, Hyden, 1983.

Miller, L.H. and Quilici, E.A., C Programming Language: An Applied Perspective, John Wiley & Sons, 1987.

Purdum, J,J., C Programming Fuide, Que Corporation, 1985.

Radcliffe, R.A., Encyclopaedia C,Sybex 1990.

Rajaram. R., Problem Solving Using C, Scitech Publications(India) Pvt.Ltd, 2001

Schildt, H., C Made Easy, Osborne McGraw-Hill, 1988.

Wortman, L. A., and Sidebottom, T.o., The C Programming Tutor, Prentice-Hall, 1984.

www.ingramcontent.com/pod-product-compliance
Lightning Source LLC
LaVergne TN
LVHW080117070326
832902LV00015B/2636